D1485126

Ancient Egypt

1000 FACTS

This material was first published as hardback in 2006 by Bardfield Press
Bardfield Press is an imprint of Miles Kelly Publishing Ltd
Bardfield Centre, Great Bardfield, Essex, CM7 4SL

This edition published in 2007 by Miles Kelly Publishing Ltd

Copyright © 2006 Miles Kelly Publishing Ltd

2 4 6 8 10 9 7 5 3

Editorial Director: Belinda Gallagher
Art Director: Jo Brewer
Editor: Rosalind McGuire
Assistant Editor: Lucy Dowling
Designers: Stephan Davis, Tom Slemmings
Picture Researcher: Laura Faulder
Production Manager: Elizabeth Brunwin
Reprographics: Anthony Cambray, Liberty Newton

All rights reserved. No part of this publication may be reproduced,
stored in a retrieval system or transferred by any other means, electronic,
mechanical, photocopying, recording or otherwise, without the prior
permission of the copyright holder.

British Library Cataloguing-in-Publication Data
A catalogue record for this book is available from the British Library

ISBN 978-1-84236-935-7

Printed in China

www.mileskelly.net
info@mileskelly.net

Ancient Egypt

1000 FACTS

Jeremy Smith

Consultant: Rupert Matthews

Miles Kelly
PUBLISHING

Contents

GROWTH OF AN EMPIRE

KINGS AND QUEENS

Contents

DAILY LIFE

RELIGION AND THE AFTERLIFE

SPORT AND CULTURE

EXCAVATING THE PAST

Who were the Egyptians?

- **Egypt lies** in the extreme north-east of Africa. The river Nile flows right through the country and into the Mediterranean Sea through the Delta, making a long, fertile valley.

- **People have lived** in the area since the Stone Age, and modern humans arrived about 60,000 years ago.

- **Around 8000** BC, the climate of Northern Africa began to change. The landscape became more arid, and the climate less hospitable. In contrast, the Nile River Valley was an area abundant in food and water.

- **The Khartoum people** arrived in Egypt around 6000 BC. They were the first to domesticate cattle and grow crops in the Nile Valley. Some of their spectacular rock-carvings can be seen in the Nubian Museum, Aswan.

- **Around 5000** BC, a series of civilizations began to develop across the world, centred on major river valleys – the Indus in India, the Tigris-Euphrates in the Middle East, the Yellow River in China and the Nile in Egypt.

- **The first settlers** in ancient Egypt had probably migrated from other parts of Africa such as Libya and Nubia, and also from Palestine and Syria. They would have lived in simple mud huts on the banks of the Nile.

> ...FASCINATING FACT...
> The earliest human skeletal remains in the Nile Valley have been discovered at Jebel Sahaba, in Nubia. They have been carbon-dated back some 12,000 years.

- **These settlers** were joined 2000 years later by people from escaping from the arid conditions of modern south Iraq. They would also have been attracted by the fertile soils, regular water supply and plentiful wildlife that were features of ancient Egypt.

- **The period of time** from the founding of these settlements until the beginning of the unification of Upper and Lower Egypt in 3100 BC is known as the Predynastic era.

- **Historians are not sure** how the end of the Predynastic era came about. It may have been caused by an invasion from Asia, but it is more likely that internal factors caused a gradual unification of Egypt.

▼ *Without the waters of the river Nile, the amazing civilization of ancient Egypt might never have existed.*

On the banks of the Nile

- **Over 90 percent of Egypt** is scorching desert, so it is sometimes called the 'red land'. Yet it also contains the greatest river on Earth – the Nile.

- **The Nile is the longest river** in the world – over 6400 km in length. It flows from the highlands of Central Africa to the Mediterranean Sea. This mighty river provided the basis for the great civilization of ancient Egypt.

- **The Nile results** from three great rivers coming together – the White Nile, the Atbara and the Blue Nile. The White and Blue Niles merge in the Sudan, near Khartoum.

▲ *Water was lifted from the Nile using a device called a shaduf.*

- **Flood season** in Egypt lasts from mid July to the end of September. When the floodwater retreats (between November and March) farmers begin to sow their crops, ready to harvest between April and June.

- **The first Egyptian farmers** waited for the Nile to flood to nourish their crops, but by 5000 BC they had started to devise ways to control the great river. They dug canals to channel the floodwater to distant fields.

- **The first reservoir** was built at Fayum, about 60 km southwest of Cairo. The Egyptians surrounded the plot with about 30 km of dykes and reduced a huge saltwater lake into the freshwater Lake Moeris.

- **The Egyptians** lived on the banks of the river Nile or by canals springing out from it. This land was the best and most fertile in the country, and was called 'Kemet' – the 'black land'.

- **The farming year** began when the Nile flooded, washing mineral-rich silt deposits onto the land. This usually led to a bountiful summer harvest.

- **The height of the Nile flood** was crucial to the survival of crops. The amount of water was monitered using 'nilometers' – stone staircases that led down into the river. The speed at which the water covered the steps told the Egyptians how fast and intense the flood was likely to be.

- **Even when the floods receded**, the Nile provided the people of Egypt with a life-saving source of water in the otherwise hot and arid landscape, without which the Egyptians' empire would have crumbled.

▲ *Nilometers were invented to keep track of the height of the river, which was crucial for the success of farming in ancient Egypt.*

11

Lower Egypt

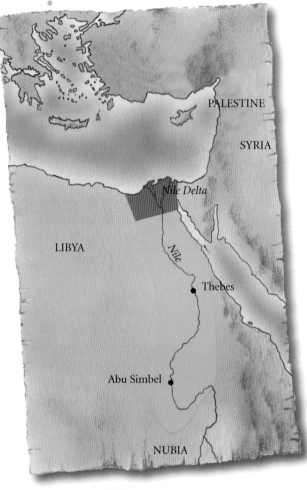

PALESTINE

SYRIA

Nile Delta

LIBYA

Nile

Thebes

Abu Simbel

NUBIA

KEY

☐ Upper Egypt ▨ Lower Egypt

- **Lower Egypt** occupied the northern part of the country, where the Nile divides into the Delta that flows into the Mediterranean Sea. Only 160 km in length, Lower Egypt was many times wider than Upper Egypt.

- **The Nile Delta** dominated Lower Egypt, where the land was fertile and marshy. Lower Egypt had a milder temperature than Upper Egypt, and it also had more rain.

- **Archaeologists do not know** as much about the Predynastic history of Lower Egypt as they do about Upper Egypt. It is usually divided into five periods by historians.

- **The time before** written history in Egypt is divided into five periods by archaeologists. Each period is named after a site from which tools, pottery and other objects have been excavated.

◄ *Lower Egypt was situated at the top of the country in the Nile Delta.*

- **Lower Egypt** was known as To-Mehu at the time of the pharaohs. It was divided into 20 areas called 'nomes'.

- **The king of Lower Egypt** wore a red crown, or 'deshret'. It was a tall, box-shaped centrepiece, on top of which protruded a dramatic looking curlicue.

- **Lower Egypt** was represented by the goddess Wadjyt. Usually shown as a cobra, she could also appear as a lion-headed woman or even as a mongoose!

- **Lower Egypt** was heavily influenced by Palestine and Syria. Pottery from these areas, as well as artefacts from Sumeria (lower Euphrates) have been found in the Delta.

▲ *The crown of Lower Egypt had a striking crest (curlicue) that curled up towards the front.*

- **By the late 4th millennium** BC, the culture of Lower Egypt began to be replaced by that of Upper Egypt. Excavations at Tell el-Farain show that by this time, locally made pottery pieces were being substituted for Upper Egyptian wares.

...FASCINATING FACT...
The papyrus plant used to flourish in the Delta region. It was used to make paper, and also bound together to make boats, huts and even temples.

Upper Egypt

- **Upper Egypt** is 1250 km in length, stretching south from the Libyan Desert to just past Abu Simbel. The Nile runs through the valley.

- **Historians divide** Predynastic Upper Egyptian history into three periods – the Badarian (5500–4000 BC), Amratian (4000–3500 BC) and Gerzean (3500–3100 BC).

- **Predynastic Upper Egypt** has been studied quite extensively. This is because a greater number of ancient sites have survived in the more favourable archaeological conditions of Upper Egypt.

- **Upper Egypt** was greatly influenced by the culture of the people from the Gerzean Period (3500–3100 BC). Based near Thebes, they moved to Upper Egypt as traders and settled there.

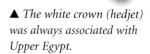

▲ *The white crown (hedjet) was always associated with Upper Egypt.*

- **Upper Egypt** was known as Shemau. The region was divided into 22 nomes between modern Aswan and just south of Cairo.

- **The population of Upper Egypt** was concentrated around a city called Hierakonpolis ('City of the Hawk'). It is likely that this city was ruled by a number of kings, including Scorpion and Narmer, and was 80 km south of Thebes.

- **The King of Upper Egypt** wore a white crown, or 'hedjet'. It is also referred to as the 'nefer', or 'white nefer'.

- **The symbol of Upper Egypt** was the lotus flower, or water lily. Three types of this flower flourished in the rich, fertile soil here.

- **An important archaeological find** from the region is the knife of Gebel el-Arak. It belonged to a pharaoh of Upper Egypt who lived around 3500 BC. It is decorated with the symbols of the fertility god, Min.

- **The last of the kings** to rule Upper Egypt was called Narmer. His greatest achievement was conquering Lower Egypt and unifying Egypt. This victory was the start of the great age of the pharaohs.

▲ *The lotus flower was the emblem of Upper Egypt and also symbolized rebirth.*

Uniting the kingdoms

- **The union of Upper and Lower Egypt** was very important to the ancient Egyptians. The capital of the new kingdom, Memphis, was close to where the Nile Valley meets the Delta.

- **The ancient Egyptians** divided their kings into families that are now known as dynasties. The 1st Dynasty began when the first king ruled over the united kingdom.

- **Records from** the 1st and 2nd Dynasties are confused. Historians are unable to give names or dates accurately to these rulers.

- **Archaeologists have discovered** a piece of slate called the Narmer Palette showing the king vanquishing his enemies. On one side the king is wearing the white crown of Upper Egypt, and on the other he wears the red crown of Lower Egypt.

▲ *The Narmer Palette was found in the Pre-Dynastic capital of Hierakonpolis by the British archaeologist J E Quibell in 1898.*

- **King Narmer was succeeded** by Menes in *c.*3100 BC, who founded the 1st Dynasty. Most historians believe 'Menes' was actually a title taken by the king, whose name was Horus Aha.

- **King Menes was the founder** of the city of Memphis. He also built a great temple there.

- **This period in Egyptian history** saw the beginning of two dynasties. The first lasted from 2925–2715 BC, and the second lasted from 2715–2658 BC.

- **The kings of the first two dynasties** of the united Egypt all came from a place called This. The site has not been located by archaeologists yet, but it is likely to have been near Abydos in Upper Egypt, as the tombs of these kings lie in the cemetery of Abydos.

- **The king of the united kingdoms** was usually depicted wearing a double crown, which was made up of the Red Crown of the Delta and the White Crown of the Valley.

. . .FASCINATING FACT. . .
King Menes lost his life in an accident that occurred while he was on a hippopotamus hunt!

The Old Kingdom

- **The Old Kingdom** lasted from 2686–2181 BC and is viewed as one of the more stable times in ancient Egyptian history. This period covered a line of kings from the 3rd to the 6th Dynasties.

- **During this period**, Egypt made great use of the vast mineral wealth that lay beneath its deserts, and gained wealth trading with other nations. The wealth was used to glorify the nation's rulers.

- **Few written records** of the Old Kingdom survive. What the rulers of this period did leave behind was a building programme unprecedented in its scope and imagination.

- **A series of mud-brick temples** were built in the Old Kingdom. Statues of gods adorned these temples, alongside statues of the kings of Egypt, who were regarded as living gods.

- **This era of Egyptian history** was one of great pyramid building. Under the orders of King Djoser, a vast step pyramid was built during the 3rd Dynasty, while during the 4th Dynasty straight-sided pyramids appeared at Meidum, Dashur and Giza.

- **At the end of the 4th Dynasty**, a new line of kings took to the throne. They called themselves 'Sa Ra' ('Sons of Ra'), and built stone temples for the sun god, Ra. This period was the height of the cult of this god.

> ...FASCINATING FACT...
> The cost of building the pyramids was staggering both in terms of the taxes needed and the labour involved. Much of the government budget was spent on them.

- **Pyramids continued to be built** during the 5th Dynasty, but they were not as large as previous structures. At Saqqara, they were inscribed with pyramid texts to help the dead king reach heaven.

- **Old Kingdom officials** also built grand tombs and statues to mark their deaths. These were decorated with paintings depicting their lives and careers. Towards the end of the Old Kingdom they rivalled those of the pharaohs in terms of grandeur.

- **The 6th Dynasty ended** with the death of Queen Nitiqret and a period of great stability came to an end. The unified kingdom of Egypt broke up into several small states as local governors became independent of the pharaoh.

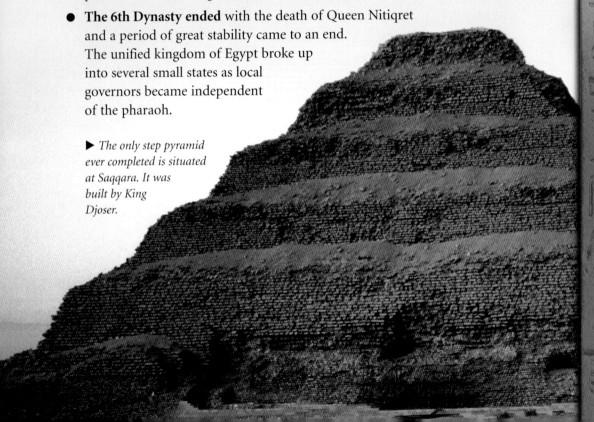

▶ *The only step pyramid ever completed is situated at Saqqara. It was built by King Djoser.*

The First Intermediate Period

- **After the stability** and growth of the Old Kingdom, the First Intermediate Period (7th–11th Dynasties) saw the power of the central government in ancient Egypt decline. It began with the death of Queen Nitiqret and lasted until the rule of Mentuhotep II.

- **During this period,** the 7th and 8th Dynasties (2150–2130 BC) were still based at the capital of the united Egypt, Memphis. However, their leaders had great trouble controlling their unruly subjects.

- **The weakness of these rulers** and the decline of the kingdom is illustrated by their tombs. They are tiny when compared with the gigantic royal pyramids of the Old Kingdom.

- **Archaeological evidence** suggests that there were few skilled craftsmen during this period. Pots, bowls and other artefacts are not of the quality of those unearthed in earlier sites.

- **The weakness of the ruling kings** at Memphis meant that much of the power was held not by the king but by governors of the different nomes.

- **The rulers of the 9th and 10th Dynasties** established themselves at Herakleopolis, to the south of Memphis. They included Neferkare VII, Kheti and Merikave.

- **After the disintegration** of the Old Kingdom, the governors of Thebes became independent local rulers. Their power soon rivalled that of the 9th and 10th Dynasties at Herakleopolis.

- **One 11th Dynasty ruler** at Thebes was Antef I. He and his successors claimed to be the 'Kings of Upper and Lower Egypt' and wore clothes decorated with the symbols of both regions.

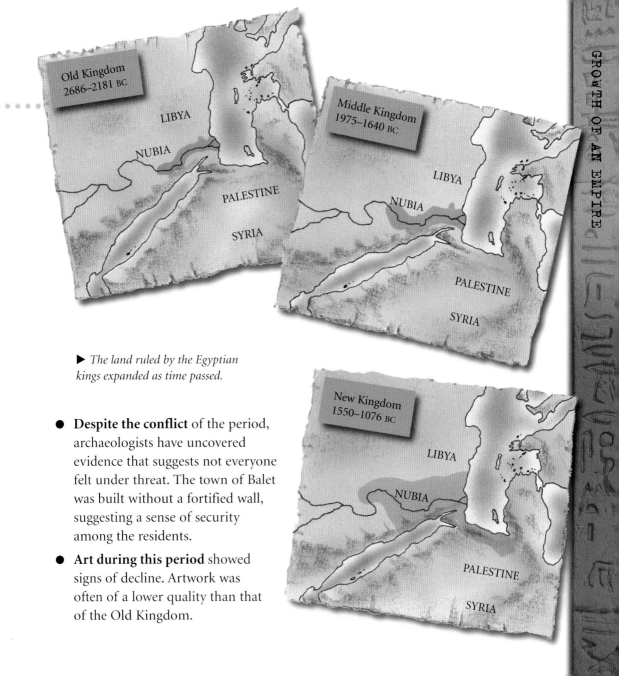

Old Kingdom
2686–2181 BC

LIBYA

NUBIA

PALESTINE

SYRIA

Middle Kingdom
1975–1640 BC

LIBYA

NUBIA

PALESTINE

SYRIA

▶ *The land ruled by the Egyptian
kings expanded as time passed.*

New Kingdom
1550–1076 BC

LIBYA

NUBIA

PALESTINE

SYRIA

- **Despite the conflict** of the period,
  archaeologists have uncovered
  evidence that suggests not everyone
  felt under threat. The town of Balet
  was built without a fortified wall,
  suggesting a sense of security
  among the residents.

- **Art during this period** showed
  signs of decline. Artwork was
  often of a lower quality than that
  of the Old Kingdom.

The Middle Kingdom

- **Conflict and division** in the First Intermediate Period was ended by a Theban called Nebhepetra Mentuhotep. He reunited the country by conquest, heralding the start of the Middle Kingdom.

- **The Middle Kingdom** (1975–1640 BC) was a high point for art and literature. Jewellery and paintings from the period are of an exceptional quality, while many poems and books of wisdom were written.

- **Mentuhotep asked for shrines** to be built all over Egypt to local gods and goddesses. He also built a great memorial temple at Deir el-Bahri.

  - **Mentuhotep was succeeded** by a number of sons, but when the last of these died, his vizier Amenemhet became the founder of the 12th Dynasty.

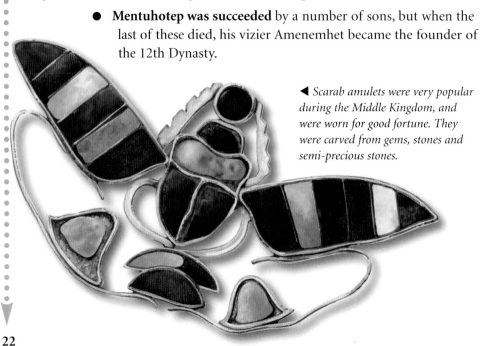

◀ *Scarab amulets were very popular during the Middle Kingdom, and were worn for good fortune. They were carved from gems, stones and semi-precious stones.*

...FASCINATING FACT...

Queen Sobekneferu was the last ruler of the 12th Dynasty. It was very unusual at the time for a woman to rule Egypt. Her death marked the end of the golden period of the Middle Kingdom.

- **The most popular king** of the 12th Dynasty was Senusret 1 (1965–1920 BC), who helped to make Egypt a great power once more. Under his reign Egypt conquered part of Nubia and defeated the Libyans.

- **The reign of Senusret III** (1818–1859 BC) saw the establishment of a number of fortresses in Nubia. A canal was also constructed that allowed boats to travel around the Nile's first waterfall, an otherwise impossible series of rapids.

- **During the 12th Dynasty,** two pyramids were built at Dahshur, and others at Fayum. The funerary temple of Amenemhet III was one of the most impressive sights of the ancient world. A new royal residence was also established during this period at el-Lisht.

- **There are few** of the great buildings of the Middle Kingdom left in good condition. The pyramids have been severely damaged by the weather, while many buildings were pulled down during the New Kingdom.

- **The Middle Kingdom ended** when a succession of weak rulers saw their control over Egypt undermined, until eventually the Delta region was conquered by foreigners. Nubia was lost and became an independent state.

The Second Intermediate Period

▲ *The chariot provided the Hyksos people with an incredibly mobile army, which quickly overpowered the Egyptian forces.*

...FASCINATING FACT...
Archaeologists have found three golden flies, awarded for valour in
battle, in Queen Ahhotep's tomb.

- **The Second Intermediate Period** (1750–1550 BC) was a difficult time for
  Egypt. Invaders called the Hyksos settled in the Delta. They were to reign as
  the 13th–17th Dynasties of pharaohs.

  - **The Hyksos** had better weapons than the Egyptians. They overran
    local forces, and began to call themselves kings.

  - **The Hyksos** built a new, heavily fortified, capital city called Avaris in
    1720 BC. It was built on the ruins of the Middle Kingdom.

  - **During this time**, the Theban kings of the 17th Dynasty maintained
    control of southern Egypt.

- **The division of Egypt** was not peaceful. The Theban king Sequenenra Taa
  was killed. His mummy shows axe and knife wounds.

- **The Theban king Kamose** erected a memorial in the temple of Karnak to
  record his victories in battle.

- **During one battle** against the Hyksos, the Theban army was led by
  Queen Ahhotep.

- **King Ahmose** finally expelled the Hyksos from Egypt. He also destroyed
  their strongholds in Palestine to ensure they could not be a danger again.

- **Under Ahmose**, the Nubian territories that were lost at the end of the
  Middle Kingdom were reclaimed. A new period of strength for Egypt was
  about to begin.

The New Kingdom

- **The expulsion of the Hyksos** marked the beginning of the New Kingdom, which lasted from 1550–1076 BC, (18–20th Dynasties). During this time, ancient Egypt enjoyed unprecedented power, peace and prosperity. Territory was greatly expanded, which brought wealth flooding in.

- **Much is known** about this period of Egyptian history because of what has been left behind – letters from kings, ruins of great towns, and artefacts that shed light on daily life.

- **With the founding** of the 18th Dynasty, the city of Waset (Thebes) became the capital of Egypt. This was to be the site of the temples of Luxor and Karnak, the Valley of the Kings and the Valley of the Queens.

- **The first ruler** of the new dynasty, Ahmose, followed up his victory over the Hyksos by pursuing them into Palestine and Syria, and taking territory there, before consolidating the northern borders of Egypt.

- **Ahmose's successors**, Amenhotep I and Thutmose I built on his great military victories. The Egyptian empire grew to include parts of Palestine, Syria and most of Nubia.

- **Egypt's most successful warrior king** was Thutmose II. He led his army on 17 campaigns, conquering cities and forcing them to pay tribute (taxes) to Egypt in return for mercy.

- **The tribute** that flowed into Egypt made the empire the wealthiest on Earth, and allowed the pharaohs to build even more temples. Mud-brick buildings were torn down and replaced with great stone structures.

- **The pharaohs of the 19th Dynasty** were descended from a vizier called Ramesses. Sety 1 protected the empire from a neighbouring race called the Hittites. His son, Ramesses II, became one of Egypt's most famous pharaohs.

● **Towards the end of the dynasty**, central power began to weaken again. Such was the religious hold of the high priest Herihor that he even claimed royal powers!

● **The kings of the 20th Dynasty** faced an onslaught from many directions, including the Libyans and Sea Peoples. Although Ramesses III repelled these invaders, much of the empire was lost and Egypt was greatly weakened.

◀ *Also called Ramesses the Great, Ramesses II lived to the age of 96, and was said to have had 200 wives, 60 daughters and 96 sons.*

The Third Intermediate Period

- **After the fall** of the 20th Dynasty, the kings of Egypt retreated to the Delta. They had little control over the south of the country. Smendes (1069–1043 BC) became the first king of the 21st Dynasty after the death of Ramesses XI in 1070 BC.

- **Power in Egypt** was divided between the high priests of the god Amun at Thebes in the south, and the kings of the 21st Dynasty (1070–945 BC) at Tanis in the north in Lower Egypt.

- **In the 10th century** BC, the 22nd Dynasty began in the north. Instigated by Sheshonq I (945–924 BC) of Libyan descent, these kings established a powerbase to the east of the Delta, so Thebes became less important.

- **The new rulers** brought statues and obelisks (tall tapering stone pillars) from other sites in Egypt. Archaeologists have also uncovered many gold and silver treasures in their tombs.

- **Under the rule of Takelot II** (850–825 BC), the 23rd Dynasty began. The two dynasties governed simultaneously for around 90 years.

- **By the 8th century** BC, the power in Egypt was no longer central. By this time, the 24th Dynasty, ruling from the city of Sais, had also appeared, in the form of a man called Tefnakht (724–717 BC).

- **During this period**, Nubia was ruled from the city of Napata. Although the country had a strong culture of its own, the people worshipped Egyptian gods. An independent native dynasty had begun to rule at around 760 BC.

- **The new Nubian government** extended its influence into southern Egypt. In 729 BC, Egyptian rulers Namhet and Tefnakht united to try to force out the Nubians, but their attack provoked a full-scale invasion.

- **In the 8th century** BC, King Piy of Napata, Nubia, invaded Egypt and captured all the main cities.
- **Piy was successful** in uniting Egypt. The various Egyptian leaders submitted to his rule at Memphis in 728 BC. The rule of the Nubian kings is known as the 25th Dynasty and the Late Period of Egyptian history began.

GOD	DUTY	REPRESENTATION
Ra	God of the Sun	Falcon-headed man wearing a sun disk on his head
Osiris	Chief judge in the underworld	Mummified king
Horus	God of the sky Protector of the king	Falcon
Sekhmet	Goddess of fire	Lion-headed woman
Hathor	Goddess of motherhood Protecter of pregnant women	Cow
Anubis	Prepared bodies for mummification	Jackal
Thoth	Moon god Scribe	Ibis-headed man

The Late Period

- **Egypt's new Nubian rulers** showed great respect for the country's religion. They began a programme of repairs to the major temples and built new structures and statues to celebrate the Egyptian gods.

- **In the 7th century** BC, a new threat to Egypt emerged from the Near East – Assyria. The Assyrians were warlike people who had tried to invade Egypt in 674 and 671 BC. The next attempt was successful, and the Nubian kings were thrown out.

- **When the Assyrians had conquered Egypt,** they sent most of their troops home. An Egyptian collaborator called Nekau was left to run the country.

- **In the absence of Assyrians to protect him**, Nekau was murdered by Tanutamani, the last king of the 25th Dynasty. However, his victory was short-lived – he was forced to flee when the Assyrians returned.

◀ *The Assyrians left behind a rich legacy of sculptures and wall carvings throughout ancient Egypt.*

- **When the Assyrians** were attacked by other enemies, Egypt again had an opportunity to fight for its independence.

- **The leader of the 26th Dynasty** was Psamtek I (Psammetichus) – son of the murdered Nekau. He led the Egyptians to victory against the Assyrians around 653 BC.

- **This period of ancient Egyptian history** was one of great creativity. Arts and crafts blossomed, with exquisite items made out of ceramics and bronze.

- **Peace was short-lived**, and the country was soon invaded again. King Psammetichus III was defeated by the king of Persia, and Egypt became a province of Persia. Persian kings counted as the 27th Dynasty of Egypt but they were not popular and there were a number of rebellions.

- **The 28th–30th Dynasties** saw a series of Egyptian leaders struggle for power. King Nectanebo II was the last native Egyptian to rule ancient Egypt.

...FASCINATING FACT...
The 26th Dynasty included some rather unusual rulers.
One of these was King Amasis, who insisted that his subjects
worship a statue forged out of his footbath.

Greek-Roman Period

- **The young Macedonian king,** Alexander the Great, defeated Egypt's Persian rulers in the 4th century BC, and became Egypt's new leader.

- **Alexander incorporated** Egypt into his own empire. He founded the city of Alexandria in 332 BC, and then left Egypt to the control of two Greek officials. He died in 323 BC.

- **In 305 BC,** Alexandra's general, Ptolemy, proclaimed himself pharaoh. He founded the Ptolemaic dynasty, which lasted until 30 BC.

- **During this dynasty,** the temple of Edfu was completed and work started on the temples of Dendera, Komo Ombo and Philae.

▶ *The Battle of Actium (31 BC) was a turning point in the history of Egypt. The Roman leader Octavian's forces repelled those of Mark Antony and Queen Cleopatra of Egypt, and forced them to flee.*

- **During the Ptolemaic dynasty**, most important posts were held by Greeks. However, Egyptian laws and religion were largely left untouched.

- **During the Greek Period**, Ptolemy I introduced the cult of the god of Serapis in an attempt to unify Greeks and Egyptians.

- **In the later Greek Period**, civil wars once again became a part of Egyptian life. Egyptians in the south tried to rebel against their foreign rulers, and there were sporadic outbreaks of violence in Alexandria.

- **In 48 BC, Roman general** Julius Caesar went to Egypt to aid Queen Cleopatra VII, who had been deposed by her brother Ptolemy XIII Philopator.

- **Cleopatra was later defeated** by the Roman leader Octavian in 30 BC. Octavian appointed himself pharaoh and Egypt became a Roman province.

- **Many Roman emperors** commissioned temple wall paintings with themselves depicted as Egyptian pharaohs.

What was a pharaoh?

- **The term 'pharaoh'** ('per-aa') was originally used to describe the royal court, but from the time of the New Kingdom onwards it was used to refer to the king himself.

- **It was unusual for a woman to rule Egypt** in her own right. A queen was referred to as 'Great Royal Wife'. Hatshepsut and Nefertiti were exceptions to this rule.

- **The ancient Egyptians believed** that the pharaoh was the god Horus in human form. He could not be addressed directly by name. The pharaoh was the representative of the gods, and looked after the harmony of the universe.

- **No one else** in the ancient Egyptian government had more power than the pharaoh. He was in charge of law and order, trade and industry, and the taxation of the temple lands and private estates.

- **There was a long period of training** to become a pharaoh. A prince had to work on his military and sporting skills and then hope to persuade a pharaoh to take him on as his 'co-regent'. When a pharaoh died, control went to his co-regent.

- **The pharaoh was the religious head of state**. He performed lots of religious ceremonies and was the honourary high priest of every temple.

> ... FASCINATING FACT ...
> Artists always had to portray pharaohs as youthful
> and handsome in Egyptian art, regardless of whether
> or not this was actually the case!

- **It was believed** that pharaohs were the only people who were allowed to approach and touch the gods. Pharaohs are the only people shown making offerings to the gods in temple wall paintings.

- **The pharaoh** was also the head of Egypt's legal system. If an Egyptian felt he had been wronged, he could appeal directly to the pharaoh for justice.

- **One of the duties of a pharaoh** was to protect Egypt from its enemies. Some pharaohs, such as Thutmose III, actually led the Egyptian army into battle.

◀ *Queen Nefertiti was the wife of the Egyptian pharaoh Amenhotep IV. It is thought she may have ruled in her own right, as pharaoh, following the death of her husband.*

The royal court and palace

- **The pharaoh and his advisers** gathered together for special state occasions. Many types of buildings were used for these gatherings.

- **Royal courts** were decorated in gilded metals and jewels. Fragments of tiles from the court of Pharaoh Akhenaten offer a glimpse of the splendours of life at court.

- **Courtiers chosen by the pharaoh** populated the court, either relatives or talented scribes. Ceremonies were frequently held to dispense rewards to these loyal servants.

- **There were strict rules to obey** at court. If the pharaoh approached anyone they had to fall before him and kiss the ground beneath his feet.

- **Life at the royal court** could be dull, so dancers, jesters, magicians and musicians kept the pharaoh entertained.

▼ *People were employed in royal courts and temples as singers, musicians and dancers (shown in the wall painting below). These positions were esteemed.*

...FASCINATING FACT...
Wild birds were a menace in some royal courts. Courtiers dealt with
them by hurling wooden throwsticks shaped like
boomerangs at the creatures.

- **The court throne** was made of wood overlaid with gold leaf. Archaeologists have reconstructed Queen Hetepheres' throne.

- **There were unofficial 'guilds'** of women made up of the wives of important officials. They reported to the goddess Hathor.

- **Some jewellery** was only allowed at court at certain times. A figurine of the royal crown could only be worn when the king was riding his chariot.

- **Only the finest materials** were used at court. Vases and plates were forged from gold, which was considered to be the most precious metal of all.

Divine symbols

▲ *The ankh symbol was based on a representation of a sandal strap.*

● **Some symbols** were only carried by the king or queen. The ankh – the sign of life – indicated the power to give or take away life, and could not be carried by ordinary Egyptians.

● **The sphinx** was one of the most important symbols in Egypt. It was depicted with the body of a lion and the head of a pharaoh. The sphinx was a beast of the sun god, stressing the king's role as the son of Ra.

● **The lotus flower** flourishes on the banks of the Nile. It opens its large petals with the rising of the sun. To the ancient Egyptians it represented the rebirth of the sun and the banishing of darkness.

● **The crook and flail** were carried by every Egyptian pharaoh. The crook was shaped like a shepherd's staff, and symbolized government, while the flail was shaped like a shepherd's fly-whisk, and symbolized the power of the pharaoh to punish his enemies.

● **The falcon was an important symbol**. Ra, the sun god, was most commonly represented as a falcon.

● **Bees had great religious significance** in Egypt. In one myth they were the tears of the sun god, Ra. Bees were also linked with the goddess Neith, and her temple was called 'The house of the bee'.

● **Obelisks were needle-like stone monuments**. They were based on the shape of the benben stone, upon which it was said the first rays of sunlight fell.

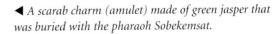

◀ *A scarab charm (amulet) made of green jasper that was buried with the pharaoh Sobekemsat.*

● **Beards were considered** to be divine attributes of the gods. Both male and female pharaohs often wore false beards secured under the chin by a cord.

● **The apis was a sacred bull**, which was chosen to live in the temple of Ptah in Memphis. Its birth was considered divine and its death provoked national mourning.

● **The large, black-green scarab dung beetle** rolls up animal droppings into a ball, which it pushes along with its head and front legs. The Egyptians associated the scarab with the god Khepri, who they believed rolled the sun across the sky every day.

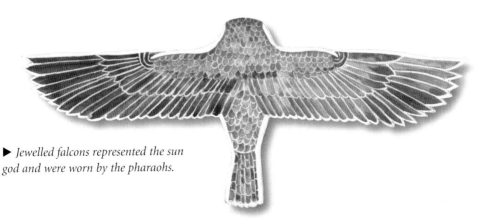

▶ *Jewelled falcons represented the sun god and were worn by the pharaohs.*

39

Menes

- **The Egyptian historian Manetho** (305–285 BC) states that it was King Menes who was responsible for uniting Upper and Lower Egypt and founding the First Dynasty.

- **There is a lot of uncertainty** however, as to whether King Menes actually founded the Egyptian state.

- **Some think** that Manetho is referring to a king called Horus Aha, who succeeded King Narmer. Narmer was the last king of the Pre-Dynastic Period in Egypt.

◀ *A scene from the tombstone of King Djet of the 1st Dynasty shows the falcon god Horus perched on top of the royal palace.*

- **Other historians** believe that Narmer and Menes were actually the same person, because the two names have been found linked together on jar-sealings from Abydos. This mystery has not yet been solved.

- **What is certain**, is that a figure who has become known in history as King Menes was responsible for founding the city of Memphis. He dammed off part of the river to create dry land for his capital.

- **King Menes was regarded** by the ancient Egyptians as the first human ruler. Before his ascension, the country was run by a succession of mythical rulers. According to Egyptian legend, when the throne was passed to Menes by the god Horus it stayed in human hands until the 5th Dynasty.

- **During his reign**, Menes waged wars against the Nubians and Libyans in neighbouring territories. Scholars of ancient history believed he was a warrior king who defeated all his enemies.

- **During his rule**, Egyptian trade thrived. Trading with nearby countries in the Middle East appear to have been well established.

- **When Menes died**, he was succeeded by Djer. This ruler became known as 'the serpent king' because when his name was written in Egyptian script the symbols resembled a snake.

. . . FASCINATING FACT . . .
The king before Narmer is known only by the symbol that he had carved on his possessions – a scorpion.

Sneferu

▲ *Sneferu's Bent Pyramid. This was one of two pyramids the pharaoh built for himself at Dashur. Sneferu's sons also helped with the building of the king's pyramids.*

● **Born in the 27th century** BC, Pharaoh Sneferu ruled Egypt for 24 years. He was the first pharaoh of the 4th Dynasty of the Old Kingdom, an age of pyramid building that has never been equalled.

● **Sneferu was the son of Huni**, and the father of Khufu. Literature suggests he was a kind and good ruler.

> **...FASCINATING FACT...**
> One myth about Sneferu tells of him ordering a court magician to magically roll back the waters of a lake so that the jewellery of one of his servant girls might be retrieved from its depths.

- **Sneferu was the first** pharaoh to write his name inside an oval symbol called a cartouche.

- **Sneferu was a warrior pharaoh**, and earned the nickname 'Smiter of the Barbarians'. A carving called the Palermo Stone reveals that he fought against the Nubians and the Libyans.

- **Another carving** depicts a victory at Maghara in the Sinai Peninsula and shows the king slaying an enemy.

- **Three pyramids were built** during Sneferu's reign. He helped to finish the pyramid at Meidum started by his father, and built the Bent Pyramid and the Red Pyramid at Dashur. Sneferu is thought to have been buried at the Red Pyramid.

- **The three pyramids** built by Sneferu were the first attempts to construct true pyramids.

- **Sneferu placed the main axis** of his pyramids from east to west rather than north to south, as in the past. This was an attempt to align the axis toward the east-west passage of the sun and so to reflect the worship of Ra.

- **Statues of Sneferu's son** Prince Rahotep and his wife Nofret lie in the Meidum Pyramid. They are stunningly well preserved.

Khufu

- **Pharaoh Khufu reigned** from 2560–2537 BC. He was the son of the great pyramid builder Sneferu, and was called Cheops by the Greeks. Khufu is short for 'Khnum-kuefui', which means 'Khnum protects me'.

- **Khufu's greatest achievement** was the Great Pyramid at Giza, one of the Seven Wonders of the ancient world. It was the tallest structure on Earth for nearly 4500 years.

- **Khufu's burial treasure** was stolen long ago by grave robbers. Only an empty coffin (sarcophagus) was found by archaeologists. Two cedarwood boats were found buried next to the Great Pyramid.

- **Archaeologists have found** part of the funerary equipment of Khufu's mother, Hetepheres, in a tomb near the Great Pyramid of Giza.

- **The untouched tomb of Khufu's son**, Hardjedef, has also been discovered at Giza to the east of the Great Pyramid.

Mastaba tombs

The queen's pyramids

▶ *Khufu's Great Pyramid, the high point of pyramid building in ancient Egypt.*

Funeral temple

44

- **A giant trading expedition** set off to secure resources for the pharaoh's building programmes. Khufu's name is inscribed at the turquoise and copper mines of Wadi Maghara in the Sinai Peninsula.

- **There were also mining expeditions** into the Nubian Western desert. The pharaoh's name has been scratched into gneiss quarries there, 65 km to the north-west of Abu Simbel.

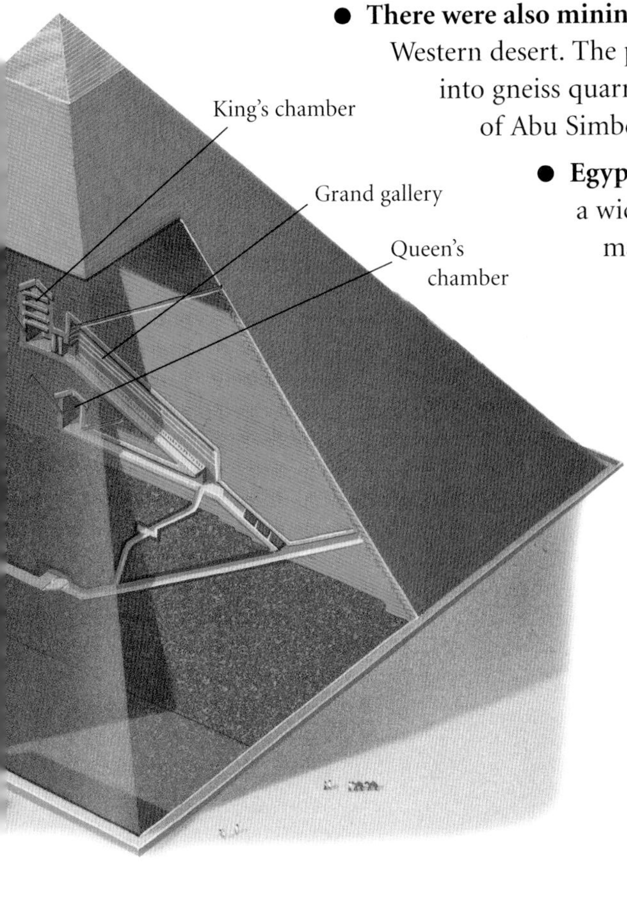

King's chamber

Grand gallery

Queen's chamber

- **Egyptian legend** suggests that Khufu was a wicked tyrant, using money and manpower for building the Great Pyramid rather than for bettering the country.

- **Only one complete likeness of the pharaoh** has survived. It is a tiny ivory statuette of a king wearing the red crown of Lower Egypt, seated on a throne.

- **The statuette was recovered** from the temple of Khentimentiu at Abydos by the explorer and artist Flinders Petrie in 1903.

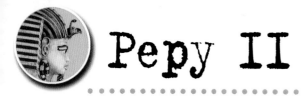

Pepy II

- **Pharaoh Pepy II Neferkara** succeeded about 2278 BC, after his half-brother Merenra died prematurely after just nine years on the throne. Pepy II was still king 94 years later at the age of 100.

- **Some records suggest Pepy II** was only about 10 years old when he was appointed pharaoh. Inscriptions on the walls of the tomb of Harkhuf, a governor of Aswan, support this view.

- **Pepy II's mother** was Ankhnesmerire II (Ankhesenpepi). It is likely she acted as Pepy II's regent during his childhood, assisted by her brother, Djau, who was a vizier.

- **Texts in Harkhuf's tomb** detail the strength of Egypt's economy during Pepy II's rule. They suggest a strong economic influence over Lower Nubia.

- **It seems that Pepy II** may have been engaged in a power struggle with some of the high officials in Egypt during his reign. These nobles had amassed great wealth, and their tombs compare very favourably with Pepy's own burial place.

- **Administration of the country** became increasingly difficult. Pepy II created the positions of vizier of Upper Egypt and vizier of Lower Egypt instead of one overall figure.

...FASCINATING FACT...
Pepy II claimed victories over Libya that had really been won by the earlier pharaoh Sahu-re. He even had Sahu-re's victory monument copied and put in his own tomb.

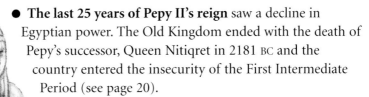

● **The last 25 years of Pepy II's reign** saw a decline in Egyptian power. The Old Kingdom ended with the death of Pepy's successor, Queen Nitiqret in 2181 BC and the country entered the insecurity of the First Intermediate Period (see page 20).

● **Pepy II lies buried in a pyramid** at south Saqqara. It was excavated by Gustave Jequier between 1926 and 1936. Inside Pepy's II's tomb, the archaeologist found a scene showing the king in the form of a sphinx and a griffin (a winged monster with the head of a lion and the body of an eagle) trampling over his enemies.

● **There are also stone statues** of bound captives in the mortuary temple. Pepy II must have celebrated victories by taking prisoners of war back to Egypt.

◄ *A statue showing the young Pepy II seated on the lap of his mother, Queen Ankhnesmerire II.*

Amenhotep III

- **Pharaoh Amenhotep III** came to the throne when he was still a child. The young pharaoh was still expected to take a queen, and married a girl called Tiy, the daughter of an army officer.

- **He also undertook several diplomatic marriages**, to Gilukhepa (a princess of Naharin in Mesopotamia), as well as to two of her daughters, Isis and Sitamun. Tiy, however, remained his first and most important queen.

- **The early years** of Amenhotep III's reign were marked by military activities, including a campaign in Nubia. The king later built a fortress known as Khaemmaat, facing the Nubian capital over the Nile at Kerma.

▼ *The Temple at Karnak is comprised of three main temples, and several smaller structures. Its ancient name was Ipet-isut ('The Most Sacred of Places').*

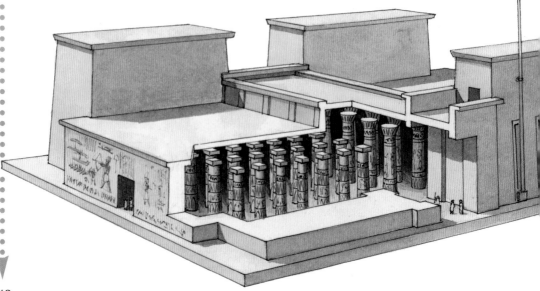

...FASCINATING FACT...

Amenhotep III may have been regarded as a god (deified) during his own lifetime. From the time of his first jubilee, he is shown taking the role of the sun god Ra, riding in his boat.

- **Amenhotep had important information inscribed** on writing material called scarabs. These were sent around Egypt to broadcast news such as great military victories or successful hunts carried out by the pharaoh.

- **By the 25th year of his reign**, Amenhotep ruled a stable and prosperous state, with great wealth from foreign trade and the gold mines in Wadi Hammamat and Nubia.

- **This wealth enabled Amenhotep** to initiate much building work. Many temples were constructed or rebuilt. The most spectacular renovation was at Karnak, where the temple to the god Amun was lavishly updated.

- **Two of the most impressive statues** in ancient Egypt are the Colossi of Memnon, which once marked the entrance to a memorial temple at Thebes.

- **Like many of the pharaohs**, Amenhotep ordered statues that made him look strong and handsome. However, evidence suggests that he may have been fat in later life and was only able to rule with help from his son.

- **Under Amenhotep III**, Egypt's diplomatic ties appear to have been strengthened. Correspondence between the pharaoh and leaders in the states of Babylon, Mitanni and Arzawa has been etched onto clay tablets and stored in royal libraries.

Thutmose III and Hatshepsut

- **King Thutmose III** was king during the 18th Dynasty. He took the throne as a child, so his aunt and stepmother Hatshepsut was made queen regent.

- **After a few years as regent**, Hatshepsut had herself crowned 'King of Egypt'. This meant Thutmose did not come to power for a further 20 years. Hatshepsut wore the pharaoh's crown and royal ceremonial beard.

- **When Thutmose finally became king** following Hatshepsut's death, he built up the army and led a series of daring campaigns in Palestine and Syria.

- **Thutmose III's most famous victory** is recorded on an inscription at the Temple at Karnak. It describes a surprise attack on Megiddo, Israel, where his army of 10,000 soldiers captured the city.

- **Thutmose's military victories** resulted in even more wealth for Egypt, and many more elaborate temples were built.

- **In the later years of Thutmose's reign** he removed many of the images of his stepmother from Egypt's monuments. At Deir el-Bahari, he ordered a number of her statues to be destroyed.

...**FASCINATING FACT**...
At Karnak, the walls record the many plants and animals Thutmose imported. Historians think he might be responsible for introducing chickens to Egypt.

- **Thutmose's favourite queen** was Hatshepsut-Merytre. He also had several minor queens, as part of diplomatic deals. Three of these were Menhet, Menwi and Merti and their tombs have been found west of Deir el-Bahri.

- **Thutmose III** has a tomb in the Valley of the Kings decorated with scenes from *The Book of What is in the Underworld*.

- **In the 19th century,** archaeologists discovered Thutmose III's mummy, which had been moved to Deir el-Bahri, to protect it from grave robbers. It was one of 40 royal mummies found in an 11th Dynasty tomb.

◀ *Hatshepsut was crowned pharaoh in 1473 BC. She was highly successful, building magnificent temples and organizing new and profitable trade routes.*

51

Akhenaten and Nefertiti

- **Pharaoh Akhenaten** was originally called Amenhotep, and was born in the 14th century BC. He was a younger son of Amenhotep III, and came to the throne because his older brother died.

- **Akhenaten ruled ancient Egypt** from about 1352 BC. At first he probably ruled jointly with his father, then later shared power with his wife, Nefertiti.

- **One of Akhenaten's first major projects** was the great temple at Thebes, which was dedicated to a new god named Aten. Many paintings of the king and his wife decorated the temple walls.

◀ *Nefertiti was the main wife of Akhenaten. Her name translates as 'A Beautiful One has Come'.*

- **Akhenaten wanted to go beyond** constructing temples. A new capital, called Akhetaten, was built at a place we now call Tell el-Amarna. The best-preserved example of a New Kingdom settlement, it includes temples, palaces and mud-brick houses.

- **Akhenaten and Nefertiti were so devoted** to the god Aten that they prohibited the worshipping of the old gods, including Amun-Ra. The king was no longer known by his original name of Amenhotep but by Akhenaten – which means 'Effective Spirit of the Aten'.

- **People were made to worship** images of the pharaoh and his family being blessed by Aten – even in their own homes.

- **Archaeologists know a lot** about ancient Egyptian life during Akhenaten's reign from the Amarna letters, which were discovered in 1888. These were sent to Akhenaten from different rulers of the Middle East.

- **Some of the letters** tell how parts of the Egyptian empire felt neglected. Others speak of plots to assassinate the king.

- **Nobody knows what happened** to Akhenaten's body. It is likely that it was destroyed. His name was left out of the official list of kings and he was not prayed for in temples.

> **...FASCINATING FACT...**
> Legal documents reveal just how the status of Akhenaten plummeted after his death. He became known as 'The Great Criminal'.

Tutankhamun

- **Pharaoh Tutankhamun was born** around 1330 BC and lived in the palace of Queen Nefertiti at Amarna. Historians do not even know who his parents were.

- **Tutankhamun became king** when he was just eight or nine years old, and he married one of Akhenaten's teenage daughters.

- **Tutankhamun was responsible** for restoring the old gods that Akhenaten and Nefertiti had banned. This made him popular with the people of Egypt.

- **The capital was moved** away from Akhetaten and back to Memphis. High officials began to be buried at Saqqara once more, rather than at Thebes.

- **Historians know little** of the personal life of Tutankhamun. It is thought that he had two stillborn children and that he did not survive beyond the age of 18.

- **Forensic examinations** of the king's mummy show that he was probably killed by a blow to the head. Whether this was an accident or murder is impossible to tell.

- **He was probably intended** to be buried close to the tomb of Amenhotep III who may have been either his father or grandfather. This spot was taken by the vizier Ay, and Tutankhamun was buried in the smallest tomb in the Valley of Kings.

- **Thousands of wonderful objects** were crammed around Tutankhamun's tomb. His resting place was a fantastic solid gold coffin with a beautiful golden funeral mask.

- **The treasures** of Tutankhamun survived. The entrance to his tomb lay hidden under building debris and was missed by bandits searching for loot.

● **The tomb lay undisturbed** for thousands of years until it was found by Howard Carter's archaeological team in 1922. They were about to make the discovery of the century (see page 190).

▶ *Tutankhamun's beautiful gold coffin features a royal cobra and a vulture's head, representing the unification of Lower and Upper Egypt.*

Ramesses II

- **Ramesses was the most popular name** among ancient Egyptian royalty – eleven pharaohs were named this in all. The most famous was Ramesses II, who lived between 1279–1213 BC.

- **Pharaoh Ramesses was determined** to immortalize himself by reviving the earlier colossal style of building. He ordered the building of numerous great statues of himself throughout Egypt.

- **An impressive temple** stood at Abu Simbel, on the Upper Nile. It was built to honour Ramesses and the gods Amun, Re-Harakhty and Ptah.

▲ *Ramesses II led Egypt into a period of peace and prosperity.*

- **Another great construction** stands at Karnak. This huge temple complex covers hundreds of acres in modern day Luxor, and was dedicated to the gods Amun-ra, Mut and Montu. It was surrounded by the thriving city of Thebes.

- **Faced by a growing military threat** from the Hittites, Ramesses II took personal charge of the Egyptian army. Ramesses claimed it was his bravery that saved his men from destruction.

> ...FASCINATING FACT...
> Ramesses II had several wives, including Queen Nefertari, to whom the smaller temple of Abu Simbel was dedicated. He is rumoured to have fathered up to 120 children!

- **Both the Hittites and the Egyptians** claimed victory at Qadesh, but Ramesses later decided to make peace. He married a Hittite princess as part of a peace treaty.

- **As well as his temple-building programme** across Egypt, Ramesses II built a new capital city called Piramesse in the Egyptian Delta.

- **The mortuary complex** on the west bank at Thebes is known as the Ramesseum. A giant statue of the pharaoh stands there today.

- **After his death,** the mummy of Ramesses II was moved to a secret place to prevent possible tomb robbers stealing it.

▶ *Ramesses II built his Ramesseum on the site of Seti I's ruined temple. The temple took 20 years to complete.*

Alexander the Great

- **Alexander the Great** was born in 352 BC in the Greek state of Macedonia. He was the son of King Philip II and Queen Olympias, of Macedon.

- **Philip built up his army** and conquered the city of Amphipolis, Greece. He plundered this city's wealth to train soldiers and buy weapons to launch new raids into the neighbouring Thessaly and Thrace.

- **Aged 16**, Alexander was left in charge of Macedon as regent. He impressed the people of Greece with his leadership, and even led the cavalry in the battle of Chaeronea.

◀ *Alexander the Great was carried by his beloved horse Bucephalus into many of the battles that helped forge his great empire.*

- **Philip was murdered four years later**, and Alexander was appointed ruler of Greece at just 20 years of age.

- **After uniting a few rebellious Greek states**, Alexander turned his attention to tackling the Persian Empire in the east, commanded by King Darius III. Its vast lands included the Egyptian Empire.

- **In the past**, Persia had successfully invaded Greece, and taken territory. This time, Alexander's forces stormed eastwards, winning battle after battle.

- **In 333 BC** Alexander's forces fought a battle at Issus with the armies of the king of Persia, Darius III. Alexander was victorious, but the Persian leader managed to escape.

- **Two years later**, the two men clashed again at Gaugamela in modern day Iraq. Again, Alexander was victorious, but once more Darius escaped. However, he was caught and deposed by his own men, and Egypt was freed from Persian rule.

- **After the Persians were ejected from Egypt**, Alexander made himself pharaoh and built a magnificent new city called Alexandria. His tomb is thought to be there, but has not yet been discovered.

...FASCINATING FACT...
Today, Alexandria is still the second largest city in Egypt, and the country's main port, just as Alexander the Great had planned. It is laid out like a Greek city of the time, with a grid street plan.

Cleopatra VII

- **Cleopatra was the name of seven Ptolemic queens**. The most famous was Cleopatra VII. She and her half-brother Ptolemy XIII ruled Egypt from 51 BC.

- **Ptolemy forced his sister** out of power, but Cleopatra called on her close ally, the Roman general Julius Caesar. Ptolemy XIII was killed in a civil war.

- **Julius Caesar rode into Egypt** and made Cleopatra queen, although she had to share the throne with another brother, Ptolemy XIV.

- **After Caesar returned to Rome**, Cleopatra gave birth to a son. She called him Caesarion, claiming that Caesar was his father. When her half-brother died, Cleopatra made Caesarion her co-ruler.

- **Cleopatra's subjects** greatly admired her, and the way she ruled the country, comparing her to the goddess Isis, also a single mother.

- **Cleopatra is famous** for her disastrous love affair with the Roman general Mark Antony. He had promised to marry the Roman emperor Octavian's sister, and his affair with Cleopatra was to end in tragedy.

▲ *The goddess Isis was held in high esteem by the Egyptians, so to be compared to her was considered a great honour.*

▶ *The marriage of Cleopatra and Mark Antony hastened the end of Egypt's independence and led to it becoming part of the kingdom of Rome.*

- **Cleopatra and Mark Antony** had three children. She used her great wealth to pay for his armies. In return, Mark Antony made Alexandria the capital of a new independent Egyptian Empire to be ruled by Cleopatra and her children, in an act called the Donations of Alexandria.

- **Antony had acted** without permission from the Roman government, so bitter fighting soon erupted. Antony and Cleopatra were defeated at the battle of Actium (see page 32) by the Roman Emperor Octavian.

- **Antony killed himself** when Octavian closed in upon Alexandria. Cleopatra committed suicide soon afterwards. Caesarion was murdered and Egypt was incorporated into the Roman Empire.

- **Cleopatra's palace** has been found underwater at Alexandria. There is hope that her tomb will be found, and may contain the remains of the queen.

Arrival of the Romans

- **After the deaths of Antony and Cleopatra**, the Romans took control of Egypt. Emperor Octavian made himself pharaoh.

- **Greek and Egyptian** continued to be the main languages of ancient Egypt, but Roman law was widely implemented. Egyptian farmers were heavily taxed and much of their produce went to Rome.

- **The Romans mined gold** and precious stones from the desert to provide wealth for their growing empire.

- **Egypt was important** to the Romans because the land produced so much food. Much of this, especially wheat for bread, was collected as taxes and sent to Rome.

▶ *Later in his reign, Octavian took the name Augustus, which means 'respected one'.*

- **Life for the poor** was often very harsh in Roman-controlled Egypt. There were several uprisings, including a revolt of the Jews in AD115–117.

- **Many Romans settled in Egypt**. Some adopted Egyptian culture, such as the worship of the old gods and goddesses.

- **People buried during this period** would have normally been placed in an Egyptian-style coffin, but with a Roman-style portrait instead of a mummy mask. These were supposed to help the person's spirit to identify the body to which it belonged.

- **Archaeologists have uncovered** lots of letters from the Roman period of Egyptian history. These letters give us information about people's lives, their worries about high taxes, and how they missed their relatives back in Rome.

- **The Romans built temples**. Names of emperors such as Augustus (Octavian), and Tiberius are inscribed on the walls of temples at Dakka and Dendera. They also tried to repair Egyptian monuments, including the Colossi of Memnon at Thebes.

. . . FASCINATING FACT . . .
Tourism became popular at this time. Graffiti describes how people liked to visit the ancient monuments of Memphis and Thebes.

Christian Egypt

- **Some historians** believe that Christianity was established in Egypt by Mark the Evangelist around AD 33.

- **By AD 200,** Alexandria was one of the great Christian centres in the world. The Christian teachers Clement of Alexandria and Origen set up a school there in the late 2nd century AD to teach Christian ideas.

- **The form of Christianity** that emerged became known as Coptic Christianity. It still survives today, and Egyptian monks continue to practise the religion in monasteries.

- **The shields of early Christians** had illustrations of the god Horus on horseback, representing Christian warrior saints such as St George and St Menas.

- **Once the new religion** had spread throughout the empire, the old pagan temples became churches or monasteries, or were left to fall into ruin. Some were turned into houses.

- **One of St Mark's first converts** in Alexandria was a simple shoemaker called Anianus. He went on to become a bishop of Alexandria.

- **The ancient Egyptians** shared some beliefs with the Christian religion, including the death and resurrection of a god, the judgement of souls and the concept of an afterlife.

- **Early Christians** faced terrible persecution in Roman-ruled Egypt. In AD 64 Emperor Nero blamed his Christian subjects for the Great fire of Rome, and made it an offence to profess the Christian faith. Many Christians were arrested, tortured and killed because they refused to abandon their beliefs and worship the state gods.

- **During the rule of Emperor Diocletian**, 284 Egyptians Christians were executed in a single year. After that, persecutions started to dwindle and Egypt became a Christian state when the Roman Empire converted to Christianity under Constantine in AD 325.

- **Egypt is regarded** by many to be the home of Christian monasticism. The anonymous work *History of the Monks in Egypt* says 'There is no town or village in Egypt or the Thebaid that is not surrounded by hermitages as if by walls, and the people depend on their prayers as if on God Himself... Through them the world is kept in being'.

▶ *Emperor Constantine had a vision in which he was told that he should conquer new lands on behalf of Jesus Christ. He made his warriors carry Christ's emblem on their shields.*

65

Muslim and Ottoman Egypt

- **Arab armies conquered Egypt** in the 7th century AD. Their immense skill on horseback meant that they were easily a match for the Roman forces.

- **Islam was made the state religion** of Egypt, and the new city of el-Qahira became the capital, Cairo. A succession of Muslim leaders (caliphs) were appointed to rule according to the law of god. These were the Umayyads (AD 658–750), Abbasids (AD 750–868), Tulunids (AD 868–905), Ikhitids (AD 905–969) and Fatimids (AD 969–1171).

- **In 1171** Salah-ed-Din (Saladin) took control of Egypt by force. He made himself sultan and founded the Ayyubid dynasty (1171–1250).

- **Saladin was a great warlord** who defended Muslim Egypt from the Christian crusaders, reconquering most of Syria and Palestine. He was a fierce warrior, but he was also known for his mercy during the crusades. His nephew, Sultan al-Kamil, who reigned from 1218–1238, successfully defended Egypt against a Christian attack in 1218–1221.

▲ *Saladin founded the Ayyubid dynasty of Egypt and Syria.*

- **Men in Islamic Egypt** were forbidden to wear gold by their religion. Instead, they wore jewellery made from other materials.

- **In the 12th century**, Cairo faced waves of attacks from Christian crusaders. Much of the city was destroyed, and Saladin ordered that it should be fortified. The famous Citadel and city walls were constructed.

- **The city's fortifications** failed to reassure al-Kamil, so he hired an army of Turkish soldiers – the Mamelukes – to defend Cairo against the Ninth Crusade, led by Louis IX of France in 1249. This move proved disastrous when the Mamelukes decided to seize power for themselves.

▲ *By the end of Sultan Selim's rule, control of Egypt had passed to the Ottoman Empire.*

- **With the fall of the Ayyubids**, the Mamelukes ruled Egypt for over two centuries. This age was one of great inventiveness in the arts, and also of successful trading.

- **By the early 16th century** the rule of the Mamelukes was ebbing away. Following a series of weak leaders, and a fearsome plague, the Ottoman Sultan Selim I invaded Egypt in 1517 and the country became part of the Ottoman Empire.

- **Egypt was governed by a pasha**, appointed by the sultan. But the power of the Ottoman Empire began to decline dramatically. The age of the Ottoman Period was already coming to a close.

Colonial Egypt

- **In 1798, the French leader** Napoleon Bonaparte landed in Egypt. He defeated the Mameluke army in the Battle of the Pyramids, but his fleet was in turn defeated by the British, led by Admiral Nelson. The French left Egypt just three years later.

- **In this period of confusion** Mohammad Ali, an officer of Albanian descent, came forward to take control of Egypt. He was given the title of 'pasha' by the Ottoman sultan in 1801 and initiated a programme of modernization.

- **Ali began eradicating all Mameluke influence** in Egypt. He also conquered Sudan, Palestine and Syria – though he failed in his efforts to conquer Greece.

- **In 1831** European forces intervened to prevent Ali overthrowing the sultan of Turkey but the Egyptian leader gained control of Syria and Crete.

- **After the death of Ali**, control of Egypt passed to his nephew Abbas in 1848, and then to his sons Said (1854–1863) and Ismail (1863–1879). During the reign of Ismail, the Suez Canal was opened.

- **By the end of the 19th century** the country was in debt. In 1876, an Anglo-French commission was put in charge of Egypt's finances. Ismail was removed by the Sultan for incompetence and his son Tawfik Pasha was put in charge. When the Egyptian army rebelled, Tawfik issued a direct appeal to Britain for help. In response, they occupied Egypt in 1882.

> **...FASCINATING FACT...**
> The first efforts to build a modern canal came from the
> Egyptian expedition of Napoleon Bonaparte, who hoped the project
> would create a trade problem for the English.

- **Although British forces** did succeed in re-establishing order in Egypt, their presence was bitterly resented. In 1918, the Wafd, an Egyptian nationalist party led by Saad Zaghlul, demanded independence. In 1922, Britain reluctantly retreated from Egypt.

- **After the removal of the British**, King Fuad I established Egypt's first constitution as a parliamentary monarchy.

- **Egypt joined** the League of Nations in 1937.

▼ *Work began on the Suez canal in 1859, and the project was completed in 1867. The canal saves ships a 7700-km detour through dangerous seas.*

Egypt today

- **Egypt became a republic** on 18 June 1953, when King Farouk was forced to abdicate. Colonel Gamel Abdel Nasser was made prime minister, and later, president.

- **President Nasser** embarked on a series of ambitious projects including the construction of the Aswan High Dam, funded by money raised by the nationalization of the Suez Canal. Completed in 1970, it controls the Nile's annual floods and provides about half of Egypt's power supply.

▼ *The bustling city of Cairo today is home to over 15 million people. Its official name is Al-Qahirah.*

- **In 1958**, Egypt founded the United Arab Republic with Yemen and Syria to resist Israeli influence in the Middle East. In 1967 they engaged in the Six Day War with Israel. Israel destroyed the Egyptian air force, captured Sinai and closed the Suez Canal.

- **After the Six Day War**, Egypt was forced to recognize the state of Israel. Egypt's occupied regions were returned. An uneasy truce lasted until the death of Nasser in 1970.

- **Nasser's successor**, Anwar al-Sadat launched a lightning attack against Israeli occupiers in Sinai in 1973, on the Jewish holiday of Yom Kippur. The Egyptians were forced back, but the ceasefire agreement that was reached later favoured Egypt.

- **From 1977**, President Sadat began peace moves with Israel. In 1978 a historic deal called the Camp David Agreement was signed. Israel agreed to withdraw from Sinai, and Egypt officially recognized Israel.

- **Many people in Egypt** were unhappy with the Camp David Agreement, and on 6 October 1981, Sadat was assassinated. His successor, Hosni Mubarak, has been in power ever since, despite numerous attempts on his life.

- **Under Mubarak**, Egypt has become close to the West. Egypt sent 35,000 troops to fight against Iraq in the Gulf War.

- **In recent years**, Egypt has been targeted by Islamic fundamentalists. In 1997 a bus of holiday-makers was fired on as it visited the temple of Hatshepsut, one of the main historic sites at the town of Luxor in southern Egypt.

- **Despite such unrest**, Egypt continues to thrive, and the economy is booming too. In 2000 Egypt signed a billion dollar deal with Lebanon and Syria to develop a pipeline transporting Egyptian gas.

Food and drink

- **Most of what we know** about the diet of the ancient Egyptians comes from scenes painted in private tombs, and from the remains of food found in burial complexes.

- **It is likely that most Egyptians** enjoyed a good diet. Although their crops were sometimes struck by plagues of locusts and other pests, the average table would have boasted food including meats, fish, vegetables and fruits.

▲ *Wall art in temples and tombs depicts rich Egyptians enjoying delicacies such as butter, cheese, fowl, and beef.*

- **Meat that was eaten includes** sheep, poultry, oxen and wild animals such as antelope. It was expensive, and the poor often ate fish instead. Some also went hunting or fowling.

- **Spice was an important feature** of an Egyptian feast. The world's major trading routes passed through the country, bringing exotic eastern spices.

- **The Egyptians grew grapes** that they both ate and made into wine. Wine could also be made from dates. Beer made from barley was more widely available, and was thick and gloopy.

- **Dates and honey** were used as sweeteners. Bees were kept in pottery hives, and the Egyptians thought of them as tiny birds rather than as insects.

- **Bread formed the staple diet** of most Egyptians. Wall paintings show workers placing loaves into flat round moulds to bake them. Cakes were also made using fruits such as dates and figs.

- **The kitchen was often a corner of the courtyard** or on the flat roof. Ancient Egyptians cooked in clay ovens or charcoal fires. Food was baked, boiled, stewed, fried, grilled or roasted.

- **An ancient papyrus** casts some light on what Egyptians considered to be special foods to eat. *The Story of the Shipwrecked Sailor* reveals that the hero delighted in figs, grapes, cucumbers, fish and birds.

- **Kitchen utensils** included storage jars, bowls, pots, pans, ladles, sieves and whisks. Ordinary Egyptians used dishes made from clay, while the rich used ones made from gold, silver or bronze.

▼ *During banquets, guests were entertained by dancers, musicians and acrobats.*

Fashion

- **The ancient Egyptians took** a great deal of care over their appearance. They cut their hair short to cope with the heat and the wealthy dressed up in black wigs made from wool or human hair for special occasions.

- **Make-up was used** by both rich and poor. Men and women applied kohl as eyeliner, and powdered ochre was used to flush the cheeks. Archaeologists have discovered many exquisitely carved make-up containers.

▲ *Egyptian clothing was light and loose-fitting, because of the scorching climate.*

- **Fashion-conscious Egyptians** could study themselves in mirrors made from polished copper or bronze. Good glass was very scarce.

- **Most ancient Egyptians wore jewellery.** The poor wore rings and bracelets of cheap metals and coloured clay. The rich wore gold and precious stones.

- **The hot climate** dictated that clothing was light and loose-fitting, made from linen. Egyptian men wore linen loin cloths or kilts, fastened round the waist, while women wore long, tunic-type dresses.

- **Shoes were often made of papyrus.** They were usually simple sandals similar to flip-flops, and were worn by people of all classes.

...FASCINATING FACT...
Women and priests removed body hair with tweezers. Egyptian barbers used bronze or copper razors.

- **Cleanliness was extremely important** for Egyptian women. Wealthier women used a cleansing paste of water combined with natron, a compound found in sodium bicarbonate and sodium carbonate.

- **Egyptian women rubbed oils into their skin** after washing, possibly fragranced with frankincense or myrrh. Poorer women were often supplied with oils as part of their wages.

- **Influences from the Middle East** probably led to ear piercing. By the 14th century BC, many Egyptian men and women wore large earrings.

▼ *Both men and women used black eye paint – kohl – and ochre to add colour to their cheeks.*

Women in society

- **All the most important posts** in ancient Egypt were filled by men. Women were expected to provide a stable family environment.
- **Women performed many of the agricultural tasks** in ancient Egypt.

▼ *A non-royal Egyptian woman was referred to as the 'mistress of the house'. Richer households had servants to help with tasks ranging from getting dressed to cleaning.*

- **Egyptian women** were usually free to go about in public without the company of an escort. They were not required by law to wear veils.

- **There were several ways for Egyptian women** to acquire possessions and property. Usually they were given as gifts or were inherited from parents or from a husband.

- **Under Egyptian property law**, a woman had claim to one-third of all the property the couple had built up since they were married.

- **If a woman brought private property** to a marriage it remained hers, although the husband often had free use of it. In the event of divorce her property had to be returned to her, plus any divorce settlement.

- **Women enjoyed a degree of legal protection** after marriage that was almost unrivalled in the ancient world. If a wife was badly treated, she could divorce her husband. She was then free to marry again.

- **Women played many roles in society**. At the highest end of the social scale they could be pharaohs, dowager queens and regents. Most ordinary women were expected to look after the family and the home, but some acted as housekeepers, servants, workers or skilled labourers.

- **Women were not usually taught** how to read and write. Only between one and five percent of women were literate between the Old Kingdom and the Late Period.

...FASCINATING FACT...
Women could be national heroines. Queen Ahhotep of the
18th Dynasty became a legend for saving Egypt from the Hyksos,
receiving Egypt's highest military decoration at least three times.

Family and marriage

- **Family was the centre** of ancient Egyptian life. Tomb paintings show different generations of Egyptians sharing a home together. Servants and slaves were often considered to be part of the family in wealthy homes.

- **The head of the household** was always a man. He was in charge of financial matters and discipline. His wife was called the 'mistress of the house' and was responsible for the daily running of the household.

- **Marriage in ancient Egypt** was quite informal. No legal ceremony was required, and it was not until the Late Period that marriage contracts came into existence. A couple simply moved in together if both families agreed.

- **Marriages usually took place** between people of the same social class. There seem to have been few restrictions with regards to race or nationality. Unions between northern Egyptians and Nubians, or even with people from distant countries are recorded.

- **Children were central** to family life, and married couples were expected to have several children.

- **If a baby died**, the family mourned, and sometimes buried it under the house. Some Egyptian houses were fitted with false doors called *mastabas* to allow the spirits of the dead to come and visit.

> ....FASCINATING FACT....
> The elderly were treated with great respect. Small figures of dead ancestors were often kept around the house to keep their memory alive.

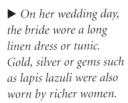

▶ *On her wedding day, the bride wore a long linen dress or tunic. Gold, silver or gems such as lapis lazuli were also worn by richer women.*

- **It was common practice** for a prospective husband to pay a sum of money to the bride's father. Later this practice was reversed, and the father of the bride paid the future husband for the upkeep of his daughter.

- **Girls from poor families** married as early as 12. Boys were usually working before they married, so rarely wed before the age of 15. In royal marriages, the participants were often much younger. Tutankhamun married when he was around eight or nine years old.

- **Many portraits, statues and wall paintings** suggest that ordinary Egyptians settled down in lifelong marriages to only one partner.

Children

- **Children were considered a blessing** in ancient Egypt. If a couple could not have their own children, they could try to adopt orphans.

- **Children were important** because of belief in the afterlife. Family members needed to ensure their funeral rites would be carried out exactly. Children would also look after aged parents.

- **Life for a child** was precarious. Disease and accidents claimed the lives of one out of every two or three births. To compensate, families had on average four to six children, and some had as many as 15.

▼ *Toys and games have been found by archaeologists, as well as paintings showing children playing.*

- **The ancient Egyptians** had tests for determining a woman's fertility and even for finding out the sex of an unborn child. They believed that a woman should sprinkle her own urine onto emmer wheat and barley. If the barley grew, it was thought that her child would be a boy. If the emmer grew, the child would be a girl. If neither grew, the woman would not have children.

- **Childbirth was dangerous**, and many women died during it. In the tomb of King Horemheb at Saqqara, the remains of his queen, Mutnodjmet, were found to contain the bones of a full term foetus. It is likely that she died as a result of a problem during pregnancy.

- **The chief goddess of pregnancy** and childbirth was the hippopotamus goddess, Taweret. Women would put an ivory wand on their stomachs to ask for her help during childbirth.

- **A child was usually named immediately** and then registered with the Egyptian authorities. Some names were a few letters long, while others represented a phrase. Many children were also named after gods.

- **Babies were nursed by their mothers** for about three years, carried around in a sling around her neck to allow her to carry on working.

- **From the age of five**, children were expected to begin helping their parents to earn a living or run the household – assisting with the harvest or running errands. Young boys' heads were shaved, except for a ponytail worn to one side. When they reached the age of twelve this was shaved off and they were allowed to grow their hair. From this age, boys were considered old enough to do adult work on the family estates. Girls helped around the house.

- **In the very poorest families**, the fate of children was not so pleasant. They might be given away to work in temples or even sold as slaves.

Education

- **Few Egyptians** received any formal education. Most were illiterate, and received vocational training aimed at preparing them for their future employment. Skills such as carpentry were passed on through generations.

- **Schooling was very expensive**, and many families were unable to afford it. The ability to read and write could sometimes lead to being given a position as a scribe, which was one of the most coveted jobs in Egypt.

▼ *Learning how to write was a very laborious process that was restricted to children from only the richest families. Would-be scribes were sent to special schools to learn their trade.*

- **To become a scribe**, you went to a special school at the age of about nine. Training took between 7 and 12 years to complete. Only then were scribes allowed to write on papyrus scrolls.

- **Students made their own brushes** and colours and copied out long lists of words and phrases. They then progressed to copying whole texts.

- **The texts** were usually moral works, packed full of advice about how a young Egyptian should behave.

- **There were many employment options** for scribes. You could seek work in a temple, a law court, within the government, or as a travelling war reporter with the Egyptian army.

- **The ancient Egyptians** believed that writing was sacred – a skill given to them by the god of wisdom, Thoth.

- **Schools were attached to temples** and government offices. Royal children had their own schools inside palaces.

- **Education seems to have been** almost entirely restricted to men. There is evidence of only one girl being taught to read and write – a 20th Dynasty letter from a man to his son says, 'You shall see that daughter of Khonsumose and let her make a letter and send it to me.'

...FASCINATING FACT...

There was no set number of years at school. One man recorded that he started school aged five. At the age of 16 he was appointed a wab priest. After 39 years he was appointed high priest.

Law and order

- **Crime prevention** was the responsibility of local officials and police forces funded by the Egyptian treasury. They investigated incidents following complaints. Police patrols used dogs and, on occasions, trained monkeys!

- **Cases were constructed** against suspects by interrogation, re-enactments, and checking records. In some cases, beatings seem to have been given out to extract information.

- **There do not seem to** have been any written laws or any lawyers. Cases were tried by groups of judges, who would all have had other jobs.

- **The ancient Egyptians** believed that justice lay with the gods, both on Earth and in the afterlife. Pharaohs maintained justice on Earth because they were believed to be the living embodiment of the gods.

- **The head of the Egyptian legal system** was the vizier, second in rank only to the pharaoh. Courts were run by magistrates.

- **The office of a judge** or magistrate was very highly regarded, and became a valued profession.

- **Egyptians brought before court** would probably have represented themselves. Any previous record would have been taken into account by the judge and the defendant would be required to swear by their favourite god that they were telling the truth.

> ...FASCINATING FACT...
> Some crimes were judged by gods speaking through priests.
> In Deir el-Medina, Amenhotep I was worshipped as a god,
> and was asked to decide many cases from beyond the grave.

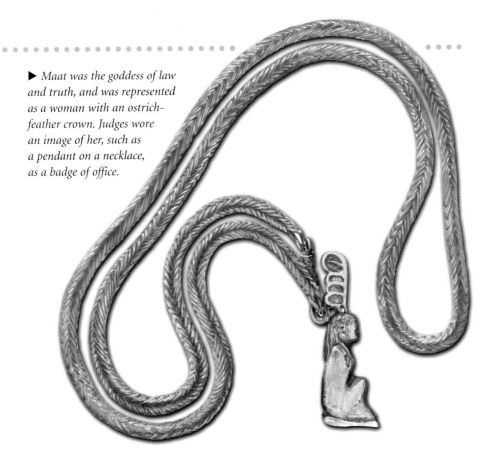

▶ *Maat was the goddess of law and truth, and was represented as a woman with an ostrich-feather crown. Judges wore an image of her, such as a pendant on a necklace, as a badge of office.*

● **Stealing and receiving stolen goods** were common crimes in ancient Egypt. More serious crimes included assault, kidnap and treason.

● **A confession was basis for a conviction** in court. The methods by which this confession was achieved were deemed largely irrelevant, even if they including beatings.

85

Tomb robbers

- **Tomb robbers** were a constant threat in ancient Egypt. Grave looting probably began soon after the practice of burying the rich and important with jewellery and other fine items for use in the afterlife was established.

- **Old Kingdom inscriptions** contained warnings that robbers would be judged by the gods in the next life.

- **Tomb builders** devised a number of measures to try to thwart would-be thieves. Goods were stored in underground chambers, and entrances were blocked with stone slabs or rubble.

- **The pyramid** of the 12th Dynasty king, Amenemhat III at Hawara, had a number of blind passages and concealed trapdoors. Thieves still managed to get in through one of the roof-blocks to gain access to the sarcophagus!

- **Some robberies were carried out** in such a subtle manner that archaeologists could not immediately tell what had been taken. A group of mummies from the 21st Dynasty in a tomb at Thebes appeared at first to be undisturbed. Closer examination revealed the gilded faces had been removed from the coffins.

- **Some grave robberies** were sophisticated operations. Amenpenofer, a builder working for Amenhotep, organized a robbery of the pyramid of Sobekmesef. They collected the golden face masks and other valuables and burned the remains.

> **...FASCINATING FACT...**
> Some robberies may have been committed even before the deceased was buried. It is likely that thieves may have been in league with undertakers and cemetery guardians.

▲ *Tomb robbers have plundered most of the pyramids in ancient Egypt. The cloth rag of a thief has been found in Tutankhamun's tomb, suggesting that the riches uncovered by Carter and his team probably represented only a fraction of what was once buried with the pharaoh.*

- **Tutankhamun's tomb** may also have been looted. Howard Carter noted at least two robberies, which probably took place when the body was buried.

- **Despite the wealth found by Carter**, most of the pharaoh's treasure had probably gone.

- **Given their belief** that an intact mummy surrounded by provisions was necessary for the deceased to survive the afterlife, it is surprising that some Egyptians were willing to deprive their ancestors of this right by robbing tombs.

Punishments

- **Punishments were severe** in Egyptian society. For example, forgers had their hands cut off, and disobedient soldiers were asked to make amends by performing heroic deeds.

- **One of the fiercest punishments** was reserved for grave robbers, and particularly for those caught stealing from royal tombs. The official penalty was to be burnt alive or to be impaled on a stake and left to die.

- **Another punishment** was to be banished to a remote oasis of the Western Desert. You were unlikely to ever escape, as there was no practical way to cross the vast expanse of sand.

- **Many Egyptians believed** that there was no such thing as escaping justice, and that even if you escaped punishment on Earth you would be punished during the afterlife.

- **There were no long-term prisons** in Egypt. Criminals were sentenced to time in back-breaking labour camps, where they had to haul massive stone slabs across the desert.

- **When an offender was punished**, their family ofen suffered as well. If a man committed the crime of deserting military service, he could be imprisoned along with his entire family.

- **Offences were rarely forgiven** during the early periods of Egyptian history. In later years, pardons seem to have been used quite frequently.

> **...FASCINATING FACT...**
> A strange quirk of Egyptian life was that a thief could register their profession and declare their earnings. If a victim of theft identified their possessions, they could claim back only 75 percent of them.

▲ *If somebody was caught trying to escape paying tribute to the pharaoh, harsh punishments were given out. This prisoner awaits his fate after sacks of grain given to the government were found to be short of what had been demanded.*

- **Sometimes people were punished** after their death. King Teti's bodyguards were said to have assassinated him, so their names were scratched from their graves, and the statues on their tombs were defaced.

- **The ancient Egyptians believed** that spirits could be punished. A spirit found guilty of being an enemy of Ra, could be boiled in a cauldron or burned in a lake of fire.

Politics and government

- **The ancient Egyptians** have left much evidence about the way their country was administered. Written and archaeological sources reveal the supply and demand of items such as grain.

- **Everything was noted down** by scribes. Documents recovered include wills, title deeds, census lists, conscription lists, orders, memos, tax lists and letters.

▶ *Egyptian society was hierarchical, with the pharaoh at the top, and the peasant workers and slaves at the bottom.*

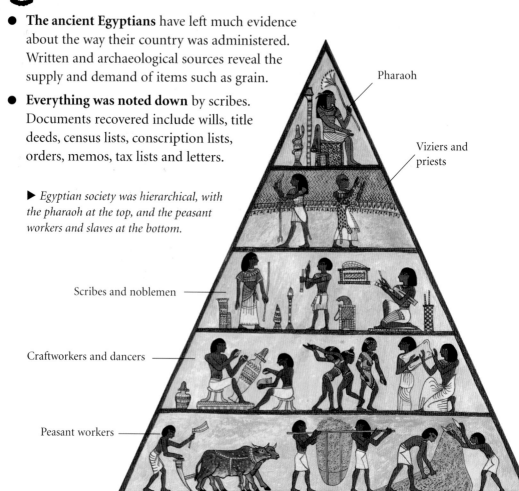

Pharaoh

Viziers and priests

Scribes and noblemen

Craftworkers and dancers

Peasant workers

- **The most important person** in Egypt after the pharaoh was the vizier (prime minister). The earliest-known holder of the post was a man called Menka.

- **The vizier was responsible** for overseeing the development of the royal monuments and for the registration of people and property for tax purposes. His titles were High Priest of Heliopolis and Master of Works.

- **Scribes were crucial** in every aspect of government, from assessing taxes to drawing up building projects and compiling war reports.

- **Egypt was governed locally** by a series of administrative districts called nomes. There were 42 nomes in total – 22 in Upper Egypt and 20 in Lower Egypt. Each nome was governed by a member of the royal family or by a figure appointed by the pharaoh. They were called nomarchs.

- **Foreign affairs were managed** by the governors of foreign provinces. Diplomats travelled between countries.

- **It was possible to overcome class barriers** and reach high office from a humble background, as noted by a scribe called Ptahhoptep: 'Do not be arrogant towards (a worthy man) for knowing his former state; respect him for what he has achieved by his own efforts.'

- **By the time of the New Kingdom** national administration was divided into three parts – the dynasty, internal administration and external affairs.

- **Internal administration** was itself split into four parts – the royal domain, the army and navy, religious hierarchy and civil officials.

Towns and cities

- **Most Egyptian towns** were built on raised land, far enough away from the Nile to minimize flooding, but close enough to allow access to water.

- **Memphis was Egypt's first capital**, probably founded by King Narmer in about 3100 BC after the unification of Upper and Lower Egypt. Little of the city remains.

- **Thebes first became important** during the Middle Kingdom when the 11th Dynasty kings made it their capital. During the New Kingdom, a number of kings were buried in rock-cut tombs in the Valley of the Kings. Queens, princes and princesses were buried in the Valley of the Queens.

- **El-Amarna**, on the east bank of the Nile between Minya and Asyaut, is the most complete city to have survived. It was founded by Akhenaten during the New Kingdom.

- **Alexandria was founded** in the 4th century BC by the Greek general Alexander the Great, who envisaged the city as the centre of his empire. It was laid out on a grid system like a Greek city, and divided into districts.

- **A number of towns** were built around specific trades. A workers' village was built at Giza just outside Cairo. It was constructed to house the men who laboured over Khufu's mighty pyramid.

- **The town of Illahun** (Kahun) was discovered by Flinders Petrie. It once housed the workers that built the pyramid of King Senusret. It was also home to mortuary priests.

- **Fortress towns** were built in Egyptian-controlled Nubia from the Middle Kingdom onwards. Buhen, 250 km south of Aswan, was constructed on an Old Kingdom site with an inner citadel, surrounded by a mud-brick enclosure wall 5 m thick and up to 9 m high.

92

- **At the height** of the ancient Egyptian civilization there were about 17 cities and 24 towns that were governed by the national capital. Their estimated population was between 100,000 and 200,000. Small towns had up to 3000 inhabitants, while Memphis and Thebes had up to 40,000.

- **Craftworkers, scribes**, priests and shopkeepers lived and worked in cities, while farmers and herdsmen left the towns to travel to the countryside to work each day.

▼ *The town of Deir el-Medina lay in a valley on the west bank across from Luxor. It was built to house the workers who constructed the royal tombs in the Valley of the Kings.*

Egypt's neighbours

- **Some of Egypts' neighbours** were a constant threat, while others became trading partners or political allies.

- **Nubia was south of Egypt**, between Aswan and Khartoum. It offered Egypt a trading route into Africa, and wealth through its gold mines. Egyptian activity in Nubia dates back to 3500 BC.

- **The nomadic tribes of Libya** periodically raided the western Delta and the desert oases.

- **In the Second Intermediate Period,** Egypt was invaded by the Hyksos people from the East. They made Avaris in the eastern Delta their capital, and ruled until they were driven out by Egyptian kings from Thebes.

- **The new Thebean kings** faced an uneasy relationship with the Hittites, who lived in what is now modern Turkey. Ramesses II subdued them at Qadesh, and later signed a peace treaty with them.

- **The Sea People** were six migrant groups looking for land in which to settle. In 1177 BC they attacked Egypt by land and sea, but were crushed by the armies of Ramesses III.

- **The Assyrians emerged** as a new threat in the first millennium BC. Based in northeast Mesopotamia (modern-day Iraq), they attacked Egypt in the 7th century BC, looting temples in Thebes.

> ...FASCINATING FACT...
> The chief exports of ancient Egypt were linen, papyrus and grain. The Egyptians traded these for silver, copper, olive oil, cedar and lapis lazuli.

- **The first links** between Greece and Egypt were forged around 1985 BC. Under Alexander the Great, Egypt became part of the Greek Empire in 332 BC.

- **Egypt was incorporated** into the Roman Empire in 30 BC with the defeat of Cleopatra VII. The Roman emperor Octavian was crowned as pharaoh.

▶ *Conquered peoples paid homage to the pharaoh by bringing gifts and treasures.*

The army

- **There was no permanent army** in the Old Kingdom. Forces were conscripted for specific expeditions, although there is evidence that a royal bodyguard was retained to protect the pharaoh and his family.

- **Until Lower Egypt was conquered** by the Hyksos people in 1674 BC, Egypt had never fought a large-scale war with another country. Most conflicts had been civil wars, or short campaigns in countries such as Nubia.

- **By the time of the 17th and 18th Dynasties** of the New Kingdom, the Egyptian army had become professional. At a time of empire building in the Middle East, it was no longer practical for the army to rely on conscripts. The army gradually became dominated by noblemen, who fought as charioteers and officers.

- **From this period onwards**, many specialized units began to evolve. These ranged from trench diggers to units armed with heavy battering rams and deadly groups of Nubian archers.

- **The pharaoh** or his son was usually in charge of the army. The army itself was split into a northern and a southern corps overseen by chief deputies. Ranks were similar to those in the modern army, including generals, battalion commanders and lieutenants.

> ...FASCINATING FACT...
> Army divisions were named after a god such as Amun. Appeals were made to the god of the province to boost the spirits of the soldiers.

- **The armies** of ancient Egypt were tiny in comparison to modern armies. In the New Kingdom, under the leadership of Seti I, the army comprised of just three divisions. Under Ramesses II there were four divisions.

- **A division** would contain several thousand men – around 4000 infantry and 1000 charioteers. These would be divided into battalions of 500 soldiers, and subdivided into 250 platoons of 50 men. Within these platoons, soldiers operated in ten-man squads.

- **An Egyptian army's tactics** were usually to march in divisions of about 50 men towards the enemy lines. It was hoped that sheer weight of numbers would prevail. The pharaoh himself often took part in military campaigns.

- **From the Old Kingdom onwards**, mercenaries (soldiers available for hire) were recruited into the Egyptian army. By the time of the latter part of the New Kingdom, mercenaries formed the majority of the forces. Slaves were also drafted, together with prisoners of war.

▶ *Ancient Egyptian soldiers would have carried stone or bronze weapons such as spears, axes and daggers. Shields, were made first from turtle shells, and then from leather.*

Weapons and warfare

- **During the Old Kingdom**, Egyptian soldiers used a variety of weapons, including spears, cudgels, maces, daggers, bows and arrows and axes.

- **The bow and arrow** was the most important weapon. The earliest metal arrowheads date from around 2000 BC.

- **The first arrowheads** were made of flint or wood, and later, bronze. A horseshoe shape was designed to wound, and a triangular shape was designed to kill.

- **Archery units** were deadlier when used with the chariot, introduced around 3000 BC by the Sumerians. These provided a platform for the soldier to fire from.

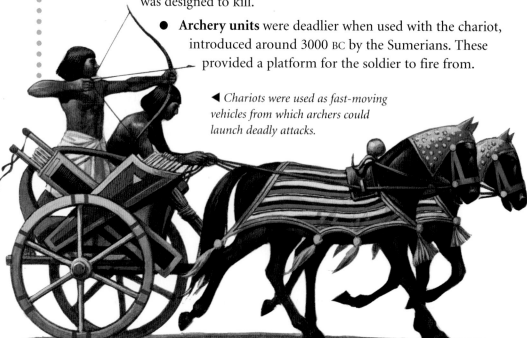

◀ *Chariots were used as fast-moving vehicles from which archers could launch deadly attacks.*

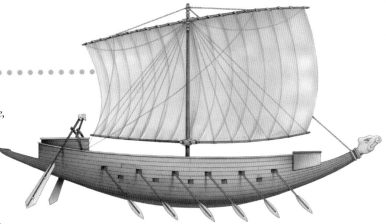

▶ *The first warships were relatively simple, consisting of a rectangular sail and usually one or two rudder oars. In later years, they were made bigger to include up to 50 oars.*

- **Operating a bow and arrow** was difficult, and specialist equipment protected the archer. Archaeologists have found bone finger guards and wrist guards that protected the archer from the whip of the bowstring.

- **The sling required** considerable skill to be effective on the battlefield. Pebbles, and later lead, were used as missiles, but the purpose of this weapon was probably more to distract the enemy.

- **Armour was light** – leather jackets covered with metal scales were usual, and wooden shields protected against spear thrusts. Pharaohs may have worn armour inlaid with semi-precious stones.

- **During the New Kingdom**, soldiers carried spears, battle-axes, scimitars and daggers. Thutmose III was one of the first Egyptians to use a scimitar – a deadly curved eastern sabre (sword).

- **Egyptian war galleys** (boats) were used to ferry men and supplies to battlegrounds. Some were fitted with battering rams to sink enemy ships.

- **During peacetime**, weapons were kept in royal armouries. When Egypt was at war, they were distributed in lavish ceremonies.

99

A soldier's life

- **Egyptian soldiers lived together** in large compounds based around forts. Donkeys were used to carry army possessions.

- **Camps were rectangular**, protected by a fence of leather shields. The king had a separate tent in the centre and senior officers had their own tents.

- **Scribes organized the logistics** of supplying such a huge number of men. An army of 10,000 soldiers would have probably needed around 20 tonnes of grain and 95,000 l of water every day.

- **Camp life** was run on a system of rationing. Conscripts were registered, then allocated rations, which they could then barter. They were paid in food or tokens according to experience.

- **When the Egyptians began a military campaign**, they prayed to the gods to protect and assist them in striking down their enemies. A mast on the pharaoh's chariot carried a symbol of the sun representing Amun-Ra.

- **There were other awards** granted for valiant service. Land, slaves and other goods were distributed among brave soldiers. Some even won the right to be buried at the pharaoh's expense.

...FASCINATING FACT...
Bravery was rewarded. Necklaces with golden flies or bees
were awarded to men who had excelled in combat by
persistently 'stinging' Egypt's foes.

● **As the Egyptian army grew reliant** on the services of mercenaries, it became vulnerable to desertion and even rebellions. Herodotus writes of the toppling of King Apries (589–570 BC) by disgruntled foreign mercenaries.

● **The profession of soldier** seems to have been scorned by some other professions. The scribe Wenemdiamun warned students: 'Come, [let me tell] you the woes of the soldier, and how many are his superiors.'

● **Despite this**, it was possible for a talented soldier to increase his position in society through his achievements on the battlefield. There are examples of army commanders who became kings – notably Horemheb and Ramesses I.

◄ *Many Egyptian rulers believed that the king of the gods, Amun-Ra, fought with them in battle and helped them to victory.*

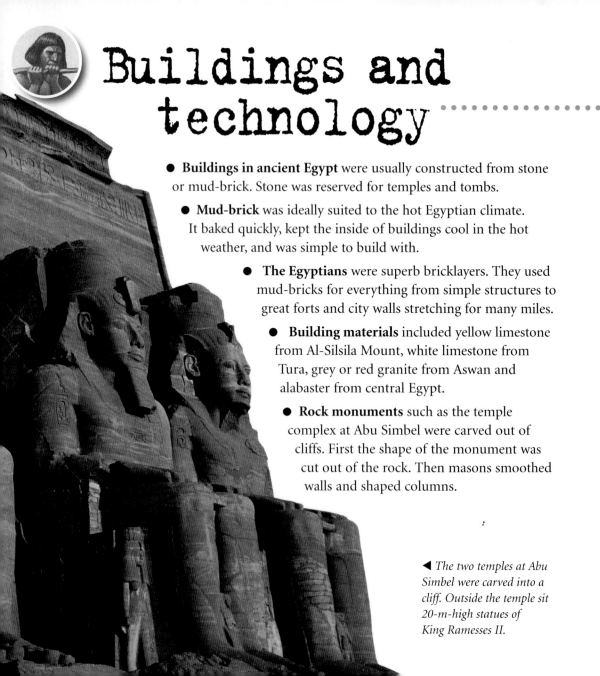

Buildings and technology

- **Buildings in ancient Egypt** were usually constructed from stone or mud-brick. Stone was reserved for temples and tombs.

- **Mud-brick** was ideally suited to the hot Egyptian climate. It baked quickly, kept the inside of buildings cool in the hot weather, and was simple to build with.

- **The Egyptians** were superb bricklayers. They used mud-bricks for everything from simple structures to great forts and city walls stretching for many miles.

- **Building materials** included yellow limestone from Al-Silsila Mount, white limestone from Tura, grey or red granite from Aswan and alabaster from central Egypt.

- **Rock monuments** such as the temple complex at Abu Simbel were carved out of cliffs. First the shape of the monument was cut out of the rock. Then masons smoothed walls and shaped columns.

◀ *The two temples at Abu Simbel were carved into a cliff. Outside the temple sit 20-m-high statues of King Ramesses II.*

▼ *To make bricks, mud from the river was mixed with sand, straw and water, poured into moulds and then removed and left to dry in the sun.*

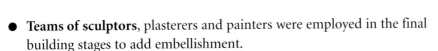

- **Teams of sculptors**, plasterers and painters were employed in the final building stages to add embellishment.

- **Temples and tombs** were constructed from solid stones using copper or bronze tools. Blocks, columns and crowns, beams and ceilings were hoisted over earth ramps to the top of sand heaps adjacent to walls. Rollers, ropes and levers were used to lift the materials.

- **Teams of workers** were employed to row boats that carried huge stones across the Nile, and then haul these gigantic blocks to their destination.

- **Masons were employed** to smooth walls and shape columns. Smooth stones were used to give an even finish.

- **Copper and bronze tools** were used to chisel out both soft limestone and harder rocks and stone, and to inscribe fine text on them.

- **Major building works** were usually carried out during flood season when labour was most readily available. Farmers with no other work during this period were often enlisted as unskilled labourers by royal officials.

Transport

- **Most ancient Egyptians** travelled everywhere on foot. Sandals were the preferred footwear, but for long distances they were taken off and carried to avoid excessive wear and tear. Sticks were used for support and also as weapons against bandits.

- **Chariots were invented** by the Sumerians in about 3000 BC. The Egyptians used these wheeled vehicles for long journeys and in warfare.

- **For short journeys** the pharaoh was carried in a palanquin, or litter. This was a canopied chair hoisted up on two poles by four of the king's servants.

- **Sledges were used for transporting heavy statues**, as they were much stronger than wheeled vehicles.

- **Donkeys were used** for both riding and carrying heavy packs, and they were kept in huge numbers. Excavations of Aha's tomb at Abydos have uncovered ten donkey skeletons.

- **There is little evidence** of the camel being used by the ancient Egyptians. It was not introduced into the country until 500 BC.

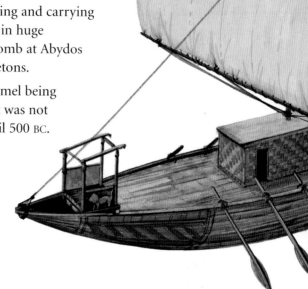

▶ *Sea merchants kept their ships close to shore. They were fitted with a large rectangular sail and only a few oars.*

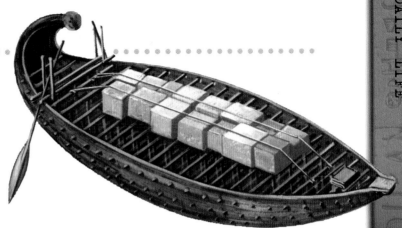

▶ *Simple wooden barges were essential to the Egyptians for the transport of heavy building materials such as blocks of stone.*

● **Archaeologists have uncovered an early hearse** in Egypt. In the tomb of the high priest Petosiris (300 BC) there is a painting of a mummy being transported on this vehicle.

● **The earliest Egyptian boats** were constructed of papyrus stalks bunched tightly together and strapped to a frame. The explorer Thor Heyerdahl successfully sailed a reconstruction of this type of boat from Egypt to America in 1970.

● **The famous Royal Ship** of King Cheops (Khufu) is a perfect example of a wooden boat, discovered around 1954.

● **Models of Egyptian river boats** show that they had small sails, were propelled by oars and were steered with a large oar at the stern (rear), which acted like a rudder.

Animals

- **The ancient Egyptians** shared the banks of the Nile with different birds, beasts, fish and reptiles.

- **The importance of animals** is shown by the number of gods and goddesses with animal features. There were cults devoted to sacred animals, such as the Mnevis bull – considered to be a manifestation of the power of the god, Atum-Ra – at Heliopolis. Some animals were given a burial in the same way as people.

- **The Egyptians kept** domesticated cattle, sheep, goats, pigs, geese and horses. Animals were a source of food, clothing and labour. The cow was sacred to many goddesses, including Hathor and Isis. Bulls were sacred to Ra.

- **Horses did not become common** until the New Kingdom. The Hyksos introduced them during the Second Intermediate Period for ceremonial occasions, hunting and pulling war chariots. Donkeys were used for transportation.

- **Many different animals** were kept as pets. Evidence has been discovered of domesticated geese, cats, dogs and even monkeys. Ferrets were kept as a way of keeping granaries free from vermin.

◄ *Many mummified dogs have been found across Egypt. Dog cemeteries have been discovered in Hardai.*

- **Wild cats** such as the jungle cat and the African wild cat were first domesticated during the Middle Kingdom. They were regarded as pets but were also sacred to the goddess Bastet. The Egyptian word for cat is 'myw'.

- **Dogs were not regarded** as highly as cats. Some Egyptians clearly formed attachments with their dogs, which were sometimes shown in paintings hunting with their master. Some Egyptians were even buried with their dogs, but the term 'dog' was commonly used as an insult.

- **There were many wild animals.** Hyenas and jackals would prowl at night, while hippos and crocodiles lurked in the waters of the Nile. There were also lions, cheetahs, wolves, cobras and wild cattle.

- **The Nile was also a haven for bird life.** It was home to such birds as the falcon, kite, goose, crane, heron, pigeon, ibis, vulture, plover and owl. Chickens may have been introduced during the New Kingdom from Asia.

- **The Nile teemed with many varieties of fish.** In some places certain types of fish were sacred and so could not be eaten, but in other places the same fish were a source of food. Some of the most common fish in the Nile were the carp, catfish and perch.

▶ *From the Late Period, great numbers of cats were mummified and stored underground in places such as Tell Basta and Speos Artemidos. Many bronze statues were also made.*

Flowers and trees

- **Egyptians believed** that flowers had special properties. They thought that their scent came from the gods. Incense from flowers was used at funerals and in temple rituals.

- **Men and women wore perfumes** made from lilies and lotus flowers. Collars and headdresses of flower petals were worn on special occasions.

- **Flowers were often symbolic** and had different meanings. A lotus flower symbolized rebirth while papyrus represented prosperity and the unity of Upper and Lower Egypt.

- **Trees provided shade** from the scorching sun. Species such as palm grew readily in the fertile soil of the Nile Valley and provided fruit, wood and shelter.

- **Olive trees** were grown around Egyptian temples. They provided a source of oil for the lamps that were needed for the many shrines.

- **Good quality wood** was not readily available to the ancient Egyptians. Most native species were small and slow-growing, such as acacia and sycamore. They were of little use for building.

- **To overcome this problem**, wood was imported from the Old Kingdom onwards, including cedar and pine from the Lebanon and ebony from Africa.

Date

Raffia palm

▲ *Date palm trees were grown in the gardens of nobles and kings as it was believed they increased a person's lifespan.*

- **The ancient Egyptians** associated many trees with gods and the afterlife. Hathor was referred to as the 'lady of the sycamore'.

- **Trees were sometimes linked** with the duration of a pharaoh's rule. Reliefs have been found showing the gods Thoth and Seshat inscribing the leaves of the ished tree with the number of years in a pharaoh's reign.

- **The symbol of a date palm branch** was used in hieroglyphs to denote the word 'year'.

▼ *Olive trees are hardy, and are ideally suited to the hot Egyptian climate. Their fruit has been used since ancient times as food and to make oil.*

Farming

- **Farming was very important** in ancient Egypt. Most Egyptians from the working classes worked on the land for at least part of the year. The growing season lasted for 8–9 months.

- **Egyptian farmers** divided the year into three seasons – 'Akhet' (June–September) was the flooding season. 'Peret' (October–February) was the growing season, and 'Shemu' (March–May) was the harvesting season.

- **Land belonged to the king** or to institutions such as temples. Field boundaries were marked out with stones. Officials checked these every two years to make sure no land had been stolen, and also to ensure that the farmer was paying the correct amount of his crop to the king in taxes.

- **The most important crops** were emmer wheat and barley, which were used to make bread and beer. Also important were flax, to make linen, and papyrus, to make paper.

- **Farmers grew vegetables** including onions, garlic, leeks, radishes, lettuce, cucumbers, lentils, beans and many kinds of spices.

> ...FASCINATING FACT...
> Records exist that show that baboons were used to help with the
> harvest. They were trained to pick fruit.

- **Fruit included** melons, pomegranates, vines, figs, dates and apples. When the fruit of a date tree was ripe, men climbed the trunk carrying knives between their teeth to cut down the harvest.

- **A good harvest** depended on the height of the Nile flood. If it was too low, the crops would be parched. Too high and they would be washed away.

- **Irrigation** was essential to good farming. The fields were watered by a system of canals, the 'shaduf' (water scoop) or the 'sakkia' (water wheel).

- **Animals were used** to trample seeds into the ground or to plough the fields after flood season.

▼ *Farming not only provided food but was also
a way for the pharaoh to gather taxes.*

111

Buying and selling

● **Trade took place** through bartering – goods were swapped for items of equivalent value instead of money. The value of goods would be given in terms of their equivalent in weight to a type of copper called a deben.

● **Sales recorded on stone** provide insights to the rates of exchange. This was never constant because the value of something depended on its availability.

● **At market places** in towns, villages and quaysides, people met to swap goods. They were also frequented by travelling salesmen looking to pick up interesting merchandise.

● **Foreign coins** were introduced to Egypt in the 5th century BC. In the 4th century BC the Egyptians began to mint their own coins.

▲ *Egyptian workers carried their oil to market. It would then be exchanged for anything they needed.*

● **Lending money** was fairly common. Sometimes these were informal loans – other times they were official loans with interest rates that could reach rates of up to 200 percent!

● **As early as the Pre-Dynastic Period**, merchants were buying exotic items to bring into Egypt, including leopard skins, giraffe tails, monkeys, ivory and gold.

▶ *Egyptians bought goods at the marketplace by bartering items such as food or textiles they had made themselves.*

112

- **The army organized** international trading expeditions. These were often dangerous. Hatshepsut's expedition to Punt took over three years.

- **Historians** are not exactly sure where the land of Punt was. It is thought to have been in the region of the river Atbara in what is now Ethiopia.

- **The ancient Egyptians** usually traded with the adjacent countries along the Mediterranean Sea and the Nile River to the south. At various times they set up trade routes to Cyprus, Crete, Greece, Syro-Palestine, Punt and Nubia.

- **Greek traders** were such regular visitors to Egypt that they were permitted to set up their own town in the Nile Delta.

Building the pyramids

- **The construction of the pyramids** was an astounding feat. The Great Pyramid at Giza was built using over 2 million stone blocks, each weighing 2.5 tonnes. The work was completed using quite primitive technology.

- **Pyramids required a site** on the west bank of the Nile, close to the river so that it was easy to transport stones, but also above flood level. A pyramid needed a strong foundation to support its massive weight.

- **After the ground was levelled**, the next task was to calculate true north, so that the sides of the pyramid could be lined up with the four compass points, probably by using the stars.

- **A pharaoh** would bless the foundations before work began. He would perform sacred rites including marking out the foundations, cutting the earth, pouring seed and moulding the first brick.

- **Ensuring the stone blocks** were smooth was the job of the masons, or stonecutters. They used tools called boning rods – two handles joined by a sharp cutting cord.

- **The core of the pyramid** and the outer casing were made from limestone. Granite was used for coffins, chambers and passages. Sculptures were made from sandstone, and basalt was used to make coffins (sarcophagi).

- **Egyptologists** have found many tools left by pyramid workers. Most were crude devices including rock drills, mallets, clamps and chisels.

- **A huge army** of workers would have been needed to build the Great Pyramid. It is likely that most of the workers were farmers who left their land during the flood season.

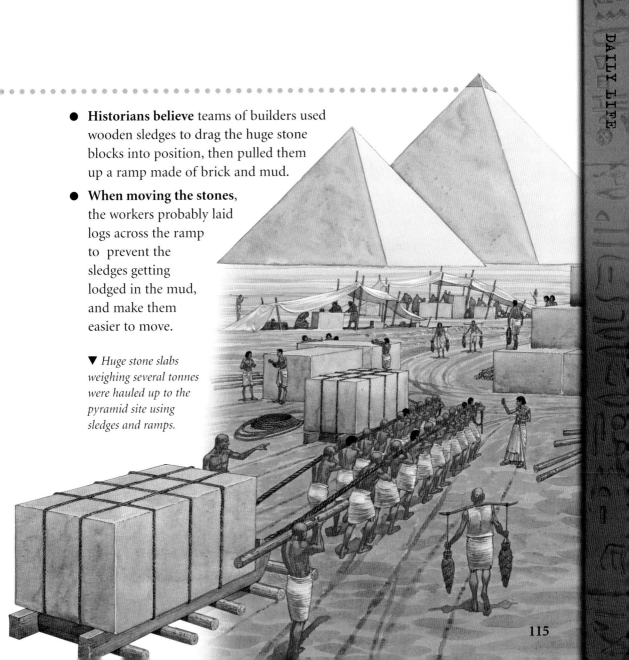

- **Historians believe** teams of builders used wooden sledges to drag the huge stone blocks into position, then pulled them up a ramp made of brick and mud.

- **When moving the stones**, the workers probably laid logs across the ramp to prevent the sledges getting lodged in the mud, and make them easier to move.

▼ *Huge stone slabs weighing several tonnes were hauled up to the pyramid site using sledges and ramps.*

115

Servants and slavery

- **Most slaves** in ancient Egypt were prisoners of war or foreigners. On rare occasions, poor Egyptians were forced to sell their children into slavery.

- **A slave had some legal rights**. They were allowed to marry a free person and own property. They could even marry a member of the family they were employed by.

- **A slave could be employed** to perform a number of tasks, ranging from manual labour to government administration. Many thousands were employed in temples.

- **Foreign female slaves** were employed in Egyptian homes to do housework or make clothes. They were often employed by the lady of the house.

- **Egyptian slaves could buy or work** their way to freedom. They could hold important positions in government, and several became high officials in the pharaoh's court.

- **Slaves were often given away as presents**, or could be left in a will to family members who then had to look after the slaves and their families.

- **Sometimes slaves were freed** by their owners. This practice was called manumission. It was not unknown for some slaves to then be adopted by the family of their former owner.

> ...FASCINATING FACT...
> During the Pre-dynastic Period, if the pharaoh died, his slaves would be buried alive with him along with the rest of his possessions.

- **Ownership of slaves** was not restricted to the elite. Some workmen at Deir El-Medina owned personal slaves – one worker owned 12.

- **Films depicting miserable slaves** toiling away at the pyramids are inaccurate. The bulk of the pyramid building was done by peasant farmers during the flood season.

▼ *Servants were responsible for everything from cooking and cleaning to helping their masters and mistresses get dressed in the morning.*

Doctors

- **Egyptian doctors** were famed throughout the ancient world. They relied on magic and medicine to treat their patients, with limited success.

- **Illness was usually regarded** as the result of evil spirits punishing wrongful behaviour. It was rare for a doctor to look purely at the physical symptoms of disease. Doctors would often work with a magician.

- **Prayers to the gods** (especially to Sekhmet, the goddess of healing) were in some cases accompanied by the injection of foul-smelling medicines into the ears or nostrils.

- **It was thought that plants** had both medicinal and magical properties. Some, such as garlic, have been scientifically proven by modern doctors to have great health benefits.

▶ *An Egyptian doctor applies a herbal preparation to a sick patient.*

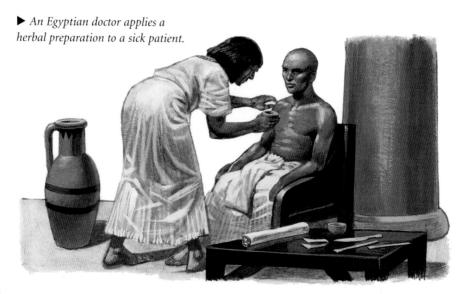

...FASCINATING FACT...
People wore magical charms or amulets thought to ward off sickness. They were also wrapped into mummy bandages to protect the deceased on their journey into the afterlife.

- **The ancient equivalents of doctors** were called 'sinws'. There were also surgeons, called 'priests of Sekhmet', and dental and veterinary practitioners. Doctors were always male.

- **Egyptian doctors** gave out prescriptions. Medical records listing 876 prescriptions for complaints such as stomach problems and skin irritations have been found, along with books that explain how doctors dealt with broken bones and hippo bites.

- **Doctors weighed** out the ingredients of their medicines according to a system known as 'the eye of Horus'.

- **Mummies** show us that people's teeth were usually in poor condition. Dentists prescribed opium to treat severe pain or drilled down into the jawbone.

- **Doctors were also expected** to treat cosmetic problems. They prescribed lotions for skin care, and ointments and remedies to stop hair loss, which included blood and fats from crocodiles, snakes and other wild animals.

▼ *Garlic was a very important healing agent to the ancient Egyptians, just as it still is today to people in many Mediterranean countries.*

Gods

- **The ancient Egyptians** worshipped hundreds of gods. Many were represented by animals. The Egyptian word for 'god' was denoted by a flagpole sign in hieroglyphics (ancient Egyptian script).

- **The sun god Ra** was the most important of all the gods. He could take many forms, including Khepri (a scarab beetle) and Re-Harakhty (a great hawk).

- **The Egyptians believed** that Ra created everything on Earth, as well as the underworld and the other gods that inhabited it. Ra was king of the gods and protector of the pharaoh. He was usually shown as a falcon-headed man wearing a sun disc.

- **The moon god Thoth** was the god of writing, medicine and mathematics, and was the patron of the scribes. He was represented by the ibis because its beak was shaped like the crescent moon.

- **Osiris, god of the dead**, represented the resurrection into eternal life that Egyptians sought by having their corpses embalmed. Mythology states that Osiris was murdered by his brother Seth, but was brought back to life by his wife and sister Isis.

- **The pharaoh** was thought to be the embodiment of the god Horus. This hawk-headed god was the child of Osiris and Isis and the nephew of Seth. He avenged his father's murder by killing Seth.

▶ *Anubis was the canine god of the dead. He was associated with the embalming and mummification process, and was the guardian of burial places.*

- **Seth, the red god**, was the Egyptian god of chaos. He was the embodiment of evil, and the murderer of Osiris. The *Book of the Dead* refers to Seth as the 'Lord of the northern sky', responsible for clouds and storms.

- **Ptah was the chief god** of Memphis. The Egyptians believed that he created the Moon, the Sun and the Earth.

- **Bes was a dwarf god** who was believed to guard against evil spirits and bad luck. He became a popular household god throughout Egypt.

- **Khnum was a god of fertility** and creation. With a ram's head and wavy horns, he guarded the source of the Nile.

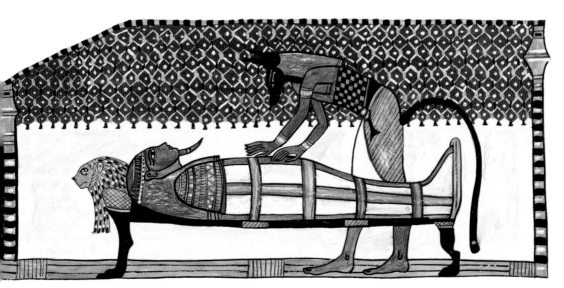

Goddesses

- **Isis was the mother goddess** of fertility and nature. Her worship was combined with that of her brother and husband, Osiris, and her son Horus.

- **Sekhemet was the goddess of love** and protection. Doctors and other healers prayed for her aid. She was depicted as a lioness and was often shown holding a *sistrum* – a musical instrument dedicated to Hathor.

- **Hathor, daughter of the sun god Ra**, was goddess of the sky and of love, mirth and beauty. She was also a goddess of fertility, and of the dead.

- **The Two Ladies** were fierce goddesses called Wadjyt and Nekhbet. They defended the sun god and the pharaohs against their enemies.

◀ *Egyptians believed that the goddess Isis represented the perfect Egyptian mother and wife. She was said to be the symbolic mother to the Egyptian king.*

- **The cat goddess Bastet** was the daughter of Ra. Her main temple was in the Delta region, where an archaeologists discovered a cemetery stuffed full of mummified cats.

- **Nut was the Egyptian's sky goddess.** She was depicted as a nude or as a giant cow. Legend says she swallowed the sun every evening and gave birth to it again every morning.

- **Nut also protected the dead** and assisted in their rebirth. A spell inside a pyramid reads 'Oh my mother Nut, spread yourself above me so that I can be placed among the unchanging stars and never die.'

- **The goddess Neith** was thought to have made order and chaos, and good and evil. Her blessing often appears on shrouds and mummy bandages.

▲ *Bastet was a cat goddess who was thought to be the daughter of the sun god. She was often depicted as a woman with the head of a lioness, and later simply as a cat-headed woman.*

- **Nephythys was a child** of the earth god Keb and the sky goddess Nut. She was believed to be the goddess of the dead, and appeared as a woman or as a small bird of prey. She was unhappily married to Seth.

- **Taweret was a strange-looking goddess.** She was depicted as part lion, part hippopotamus and part crocodile. She was a kind and generous figure who protected women and children.

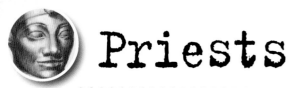

Priests

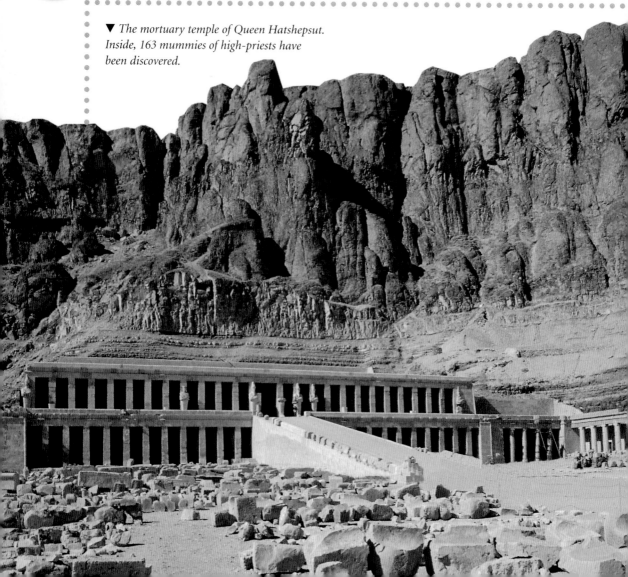

▼ *The mortuary temple of Queen Hatshepsut. Inside, 163 mummies of high-priests have been discovered.*

- **The pharaoh was the high priest** of Egypt, and the only priest allowed to be depicted in the temples. Thousands of lesser priests were employed to look after the temples.

- **A priest's main role** was to care for the temple. Scribes were usually appointed as priests, and in many cases the position became hereditary.

- **The pharaoh was supported** by the chief priest, or 'first prophet'. The 'second prophets' looked after the economy of the temple. The lower orders (wab priests) looked after more menial duties such as cleaning.

- **Documents and art** tell us that there were female priests until the New Kingdom. Many served as priestesses of the goddess Hathor.

- **Ordinary Egyptians were not allowed** inside the inner regions of the temples, and only saw the temple images of the gods during festival processions. They left offerings to the gods in the outer temple courts.

- **Priests were paid** with the offerings in the temple. The essence of these were thought to be consumed by the gods, but the priests ate the physical substance. Most priests worked in a shift system.

- **Some priests had specialist skills** and knowledge. In some parts of Egypt 'hour priests' skilled in astronomy were charged with determining when key festivals took place.

- **Priests had to wash** twice during the day and twice during the night. They also had to be clean-shaven, without body hair, and circumcised. They were not allowed to wear wool or leather.

- **Although religious knowledge** was not a necessary requirement for entering the priesthood, there were strict rules governing the profession, and priests were forbidden to discuss what went on inside a temple.

125

Temples

- **A temple was a building** or buildings that was considered to be the house of a god. After the pyramids, they were probably the most impressive structures in ancient Egypt.

- **The most important part** of any temple was the shrine, where the statue of the god was kept.

- **Each temple was dedicated** to a particular god, or a family of gods. Every day priests and priestesses would serve the statue with a selection of food and clothing, and play sweet music to it.

- **Few pre-New Kingdom temples** have survived as they were built out of reeds or mud-brick. Later temples were colossal stone buildings.

- **Egyptian temples were not places of worship** for the public. They were normally only visited by priests and kings, except sometimes during religious festivals.

- **Large temples** were funded by the Egyptian state. Some became small towns, with villages for the priests and workers, as well as schools, libraries and other facilities.

- **Temples also served as vast grain banks.** Taxes were collected in the form of this crop, and then later redistributed to workers as wages. Other buildings served as animal slaughterhouses, producing food to feed the temple staff.

- **From the later Middle Kingdom onwards**, massive ceremonial gateways called pylons were added to the temples to make them look more impressive.

- **These pylons were often flanked** by two needle-shaped monuments called obelisks. These were dedicated to the sun god.

- **The Egyptians held many annual festivals** to celebrate their gods and goddesses. People were allowed inside the temples to celebrate.

▼ *Massive pylons often flanked the entrance to great Egyptian temples such as Luxor, followed by a large courtyard.*

Life after death

- **The ancient Egyptians** did not believe that death was the end of life. They believed that if you prayed to the gods and looked after the body through mummification, you could continue to live in another world.

- **The Egyptians believed** that three parts of a person lived on after death – the soul ('Akh'), the life force ('Ka'), and the memory and personality ('Ba'). They also believed that a person's name and their shadow were real entities.

- **After death**, a person's ka would rest while the body was mummified. It then needed to be reactivated for the spiritual transformation of rebirth. A person's ba made this journey through the underworld of Duat.

- **Duat was believed to exist** deep below the Earth. It was a perilous place that the deceased would need every possible help to navigate their way through safely.

- **The Books of the Dead** were exquisitely decorated scrolls of papyrus made as passports through the treacherous world of Duat. They have often been found by archaeologists in the tombs of mummies, sometimes even wrapped in the bandages!

- **Before entering the afterlife**, the deceased was expected to deny all the evil deeds they might have committed in their lifetime. They appeared before the goddess of truth, Maat, to make this proclamation.

- **A dead person's heart** was weighed against Maat. The scales were held by Anubis, while the god Thoth recorded the judgement.

- **If you passed this test**, you were fit to enter paradise – known as the Fields of Iaru or the Field of Reeds. Ancient Egyptians believed this took the form of an agricultural heaven, the domain of Osiris, where the crops were of gigantic proportions.

- **If you failed the test,** your heart would be devoured by a beast called Ammut, who was part crocodile, part lion and part hippopotamus. You would not survive the afterlife.

- **If you failed to enter paradise,** you were sent back as an evil spirit or illness to the land of the living, to be hated and feared by both men and the gods.

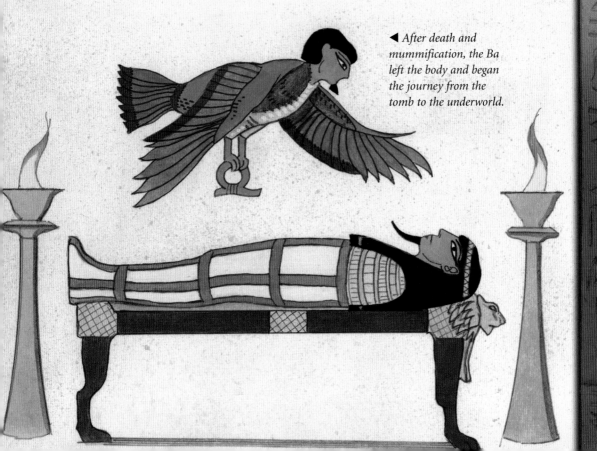

◄ *After death and mummification, the Ba left the body and began the journey from the tomb to the underworld.*

Making a mummy

- **A mummy is a dead body** preserved by drying. The term comes from the Egyptian word 'Mum', meaning 'wax', referring to the process of wrapping the corpse in a waxed cloth to stop it rotting away.

- **There had been attempts** at preserving royal corpses during the Old Kingdom, but the practice became common during the Middle Kingdom and reached a peak during the New Kingdom.

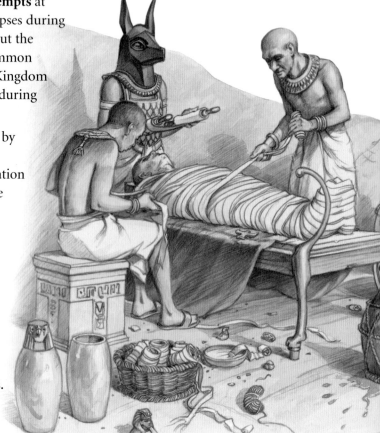

- **It was believed** that by preserving the body through mummification the spirit (Ka) of the deceased would be able to live again.

- **We know about the process** of mummy making from tomb illustrations and from the writings of the Greek historian Herodotus.

...FASCINATING FACT...

When a corpse was made into a mummy, it became known as 'Sah'.
The process was thought to change a corpse into a new body
that was 'filled with magic'.

● **The dead body** was taken to a place called the House of Beauty, where the embalming would be carried out. The body was washed, and the brain was pulled out through the nose with an iron hook.

● **A slit was made** in the left side of the body and the liver, lungs, stomach and intestines were removed and put in special canopic jars. The heart was left in place.

● **The body was packed** with a chemical called natron to dehydrate it. It was left for 40 days and then stuffed with herbs to take away the smell. The skin was rubbed with ointment and coated with resin.

● **The mummy was wrapped** in linen bandages. Amulets and jewellery were wrapped into the bandages to help the deceased in the afterlife.

● **A painted mask** was sometimes put over the mummy's head. In the case of a king this could be spectacularly ornate. The mummy was then placed in the coffin, ready for the funeral.

◀ *The name of the priest in charge of mummification was 'hery seshta' (overseer of the mysteries). He represented the god Anubis.*

Funerals and burials

● **The type of burial an ancient Egyptian** was given depended on their wealth. Most peasants were buried in shallow round pits lying on their left side, facing west, with a few of their possessions scattered around.

▼ *In the ritual of the opening of the mouth, the jaw of the coffin was 'opened' using an adze (a tool with a bronze blade). The wall painting below (from Tutankhamun's burial chamber) shows Ay performing the ceremony for the deceased king. Ay became the next pharaoh.*

- **For wealthy Egyptians**, funerals were lengthy occasions. The deceased were taken to their resting place in a funerary cortege with priests, family members and even a group of professional mourners.

- **The family** walked behind the coffin. As a sign of respect, men would be unshaven and women wore blue headbands.

- **Offerings were made** in the name of the pharaoh, as he was the connection between men and the gods. The eldest son was then expected to carry out rituals that were the duties of the heir and successor.

- **The mummy of the deceased** was transported to its final resting place where the 'Opening of the Mouth' ritual was performed, to restore the mummy's senses so that it could see, breathe and hear again in the afterlife.

- **In the Offering Ritual**, the priest recited spells to ensure the spirit of the dead person had everything it needed in the afterlife.

- **By the time of the Old Kingdom**, the rich were buried in grand tombs called *mastabas*. These were thought of as homes for the dead, and they contained rooms for everything the deceased might need for the afterlife.

- **Mastabas contained chapels** fitted with false doors. The Egyptians believed that the spirit of the deceased could go through them to receive offerings and then return to the afterlife. Food and drink were also left for the dead.

- **The soul of the dead** was believed to journey with the sun around the world. A model of the deceased in a boat was often included in tombs from the Middle Kingdom onwards to represent this journey.

- **By the late New Kingdom**, and with the threat of tomb robberies, the lavish tombs with expensive coffins and fittings were replaced with more secretive burials in places that could be more easily protected.

A king's resting place

- **Pyramids have square bases** and four triangular sides sloping up to the top to a pointed tip. Over 80 have been found, most built as royal tombs.

- **Egypt's pyramids** are on the west bank of the Nile. In the Old Kingdom, they were built around Memphis. In the Middle Kingdom, pyramids were built further south.

- **The stepped pyramid** contained a series of burial chambers for the king and his family. It was surrounded by a series of courtyards and ceremonial buildings.

- **Festivals were held** in the courtyards. In the Sed festival, the pharaoh ran round a track to symbolize a renewal of his powers before being re-crowned.

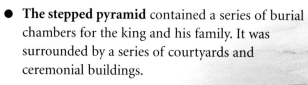

Great Pyramid of Pharaoh Khufu

Pyramid of Pharaoh Khafra

Pyramid of Pharaoh Menkaura

...FASCINATING FACT...
The contents of the stepped pyramid at Saqqara were looted
long ago, and when archaeologists finally entered the tomb, only
a mummified foot remained!

- **The first smooth pyramid** was developed by Pharaoh Sneferu. It was built out of massive slabs rather than small blocks. The steps were filled in to produce a true pyramid shape.

- **Three great pyramids** were built by Egyptian pharaohs at Giza. These were the pyramids of Menkaura, Khafra and Khufu.

- **The largest pyramid** is the Great Pyramid of Khufu at Giza (see page 136). It was built for Pharaoh Khufu around 2550 BC. Its sides are almost perfectly aligned with true north, south, east and west.

- **Ten pyramids** stand at Giza. Three pharaohs insisted that smaller pyramids be built alongside their own, for their wives. These are known as Queen's pyramids.

- **The architecture of the pyramids** has influenced architects all over the world. Pyramid tombs have been used in Europe for centuries, and the shape is also used for many innovative building projects today.

◄ *The complex at Giza contains Khufu's great pyramid, and the pyramids of Khafra and Menkaura. The smaller pyramids belonging to queens.*

The Great Pyramid

- **The Great Pyramid** of Giza is one of the Seven Wonders of the Ancient World, constructed for Pharaoh Khufu about 4500 years ago. Until the completion of the Eiffel Tower in 1887, it was the tallest structure ever built.

- **The pyramid's ancient name** was 'The Pyramid which is the Place of Sunrise and Sunset'. Its sides were covered with gleaming white limestone, and the tip of the pyramid was capped with gold to reflect the sun's rays.

- **Inside the Great Pyramid** a labyrinth of passages and chambers lead to the king's chamber. The queen's chamber was below this.

◀ *The Egyptians believed that the sculpture of the Sphinx had magical powers that would help protect the tombs and temples it watched over. It was regarded as a symbol of the rising sun.*

. . . .

...FASCINATING FACT...
The Great Pyramid contains about 2 million blocks of stone, each weighing over 2 tons. Together with the other two pharaoh's pyramids at Giza, there is enough stone to build a 3 m high wall around France.

- **An investigation** into one of the air shafts leading from the queen's chamber in 1993 revealed a blockage half-way along the passage, which might be a fourth chamber or the end of the shaft. Permission for further investigations has not yet been granted.

- **On the east side of the Great Pyramid** stands Khufu's mortuary temple and in front stands the Sphinx.

- **The Great Pyramid was emptied** by grave robbers long ago. Archaeologists did find a stone sarcophagus inside the king's chamber. It was larger than the door, and must have been put there as the pyramid was being built.

- **The Sphinx was a mythical beast**, with the body of a lion and the head of a king. A gigantic stone statue of one has watched over the ancient pyramids for over 4500 years. The sculpture has been submerged in sand for most of its history.

- **In the 19th century**, European tourists paid local people to carry them up to the top of Khufu's pyramid. Many were killed on the treacherous climb, and it is now against the law.

- **Today, the Great Pyramid** is very near to the modern Egyptian capital, Cairo, and the stone is being damaged by pollution from the cars and factories of the busy city.

Valley of the Queens

- **The Valley of the Queens**, on the west bank of the Nile at Thebes, was the main cemetery for royal wives and children during the New Kingdom. It is called 'Set Neferu', which means 'seat of beauty'.

- **There are about 75 tombs** in the valley. They usually consist of a small antechamber followed by a corridor that leads to the burial chamber.

▼ *The tomb of Nefertari has the best preserved paintings of any Egyptian site yet discovered. They depict the Queen's journey to the afterlife.*

When the tombs of the Valley of the Queens were discovered by the Italian archaeologist Ernesto Schiaparelli at the beginning of the 20th century, they were in a bad condition. Some were in use as donkey stables.

The most famous and the most spectacular tomb belongs to Queen Nefertari, wife of Ramesses II (1279–1213 BC).

Nefertari's tomb contains art depicting the queen worshipping the mummified body of Osiris and offering milk to the goddess Hathor.

Despite the Valley's name, it also contains the tombs of several princes of the New Kingdom, including the sons of Ramesses III – Khaemwaset II and Amenherkhepeshef.

Prince Kamuast had a tomb similar to that of a pharaoh, but much smaller. It is brightly decorated, with scenes of offerings and tributes.

Scenes in Prince Khaemweset's tomb offer a valuable insight into the Egyptian view of the afterlife. He is shown being presented to the guardians of the gates with his father, making an offering and dressed in a robe.

Thiti is thought to be the wife of Ramesses IV. Her tomb has now been restored, and features a beautiful embossed decoration on limestone.

...FASCINATING FACT...
The Valley of the Queens was once known as Ta-Set-Neferu ('the place of the Children of the Pharaoh'), because many princes and princesses were buried there.

Valley of the Kings

- **The Valley of the Kings** also lies on the west bank of the Nile, and is actually made up of an east and a west valley. It contains many of the tombs of pharaohs from the New Kingdom, including Tutankhamun and Ramesses II.

- **The eastern valley** is the burial place of kings of the 18th–20th Dynasties. The western valley (also called the Cemetery of the Monkeys) contains just four tombs, including that of Amenhotep III.

- **At first, tomb entrances** were disguised to prevent anyone locating them. When this practice ended, guards were appointed to watch over the tombs instead, with much less success.

- **Most tombs** were cut into the limestone. They contained three corridors, an antechamber and a sarcophagus chamber. These burial chambers were harder to rob and more skilfully concealed from potential thieves.

- **The corridors ended with the burial chamber** where the pharaoh's body was placed, surrounded by the finest treasures of Egypt. Paintings of gods and goddesses covered the ceiling and walls.

- **The Valley required the skills** of dozens of workmen who lived in the village of Deir-el-Medina. The village thrived for over 500 years and sustained up to 60 families. Its stone foundations still stand.

> ...**FASCINATING FACT**...
> Egyptian legend says that the Valley of the Kings was protected by a goddess called Meretseger. She took the form of a cobra and was believed to kill anyone who had evil in mind, or who swore false oaths.

- **The tomb of Seti I** is the longest in the valley – 120 m – and is covered with colourful paintings. The paintings show scenes of the Opening of the Mouth ritual and engraved passages from the *Book of the Dead*.

- **Tutankhamun's tomb** is one of the smallest in the Valley.

- **Despite all the precautions** the Egyptians took, nearly all the tombs in the Valley of the Kings have been looted.

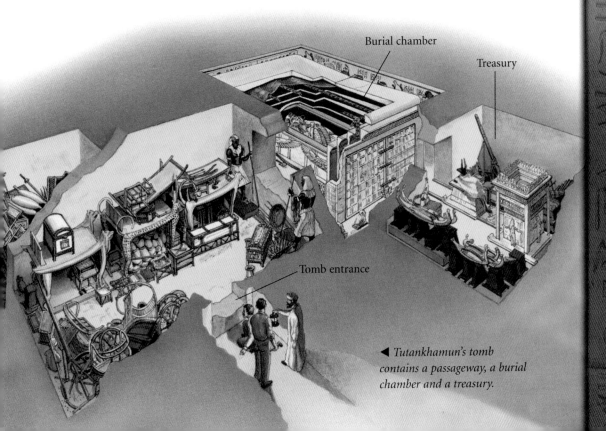

Burial chamber

Treasury

Tomb entrance

◀ *Tutankhamun's tomb contains a passageway, a burial chamber and a treasury.*

Saqqara

- **Saqqara was part of the royal cemetery** of Memphis, and was one of the most important sites in ancient Egypt.

- **It was in use as a burial ground** from the 1st Dynasty to the Christian period. Today it is packed with tombs and galleries.

▲ *Many of the tombs at Saqqara contain spectacular wall paintings, made by mixing mineral pigments with bone, glue and water to create a vibrant and lasting artwork.*

- **The step pyramid of Djoser**, built around 2650 BC, was the world's first monumental stone building. It had an underground burial chamber lined with granite, and a sealed chamber that held a statue of the king.

- **Saqqara became the resting place** for many generations of pharaohs. Kings from the 5th and 6th Dynasties were buried in smaller pyramids. Nobles were housed in tombs called *mastabas*.

- **The Pyramid Texts** were a series of beautiful, elaborate spells carved into the walls of some of the pyramids at Saqqara. They contain many references to the cult of the sun god Ra.

- **During the New Kingdom**, many important officials moved to the city of Memphis. When they died, they were buried at Saqqara.

- **By the Late Period**, vast numbers of sacred animals were being buried at the north end of Saqqara. These included baboons, ibis and hawks.

- **Most of the tombs at Saqqara** were built of very small stone blocks that were often dismantled and used elsewhere. The Christian monastery of Apa Jeremias is built almost entirely from Saqqara tomb blocks.

- **By the time of the Graeco-Roman period**, Saqqara had become a centre for pilgrims, but it remained a burial place for Egyptian leaders until the arrival of Christianity.

...FASCINATING FACT...

The most popular animals to be buried at Saqqara were cats. Their remains were placed in private funerary monuments rather than in separate burial areas.

Magic and ritual

- **The ancient Egyptians** believed that magical powers came from the gods. The source of these powers was a force called *heka,* used to create the world and protect it from the forces of chaos.

- **They also believed** the gods bestowed magical powers on the pharaohs. Priests and magicians were also thought to possess magical powers.

▲ *The city of Mendes was the centre of the cult of the goddess Hat-Mehit, who was known as chief of the fishes. For this reason, fish amulets were commonly worn here.*

- **Hundreds of books** containing magic spells were kept in temple libraries. Some priests specialized in magic. Some priests were said to be able to turn statues into real objects.

- **Many Egyptians thought** that magic could be used to manipulate people's behaviour. It was believed that a magician could use war spells to defend a country from invaders.

- **Some days** were regarded as unlucky in ancient Egypt. Papyrus calendars have some days ringed in red, a colour thought to represent the dry desert, and thus bad fortune.

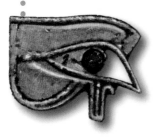

- **For a magic spell to be successful**, the Egyptians believed that it had to be performed when the conditions were perfect. Dusk and dawn were thought to be good times to cast spells. It was also important that the ingredients for the spell were pure and of good quality.

◀ *The eye of Horus represented the act of healing. Amulets of this symbol were worn for protection and strength.*

▲ *The scarab amulet is made in the form of a scarab beetle. It was the symbol of Khepri, the sun god associated with resurrection. They were one of the most common types of amulets worn in ancient Egypt.*

- **Spells were often accompanied** by a ritual. Some spells required the magician to just wave their hands, while in other spells miniature figurines had to be burned, spat upon or stabbed for the spell to work.

- **Archaeologists have found special bricks** embedded in the side of several New Kingdom tombs. These were sets of four mud-bricks that the Egyptians believed were magical, and would protect the deceased from evil.

- **Each magic brick** held a specific object – an amulet, an Anubis or a shabti figure. Text from the *Book of the Dead* was inscribed on the bricks to defend the deceased from the enemies of Osiris.

...FASCINATING FACT...
Magic wands were made of bronze or ivory. Sometimes
they were shaped like snakes because the goddess of magic,
Selket, was depicted as a snake.

Dreams

- **The ancient Egyptians believed** that dreams held great power and called them 'revelations of the truth'. They were seen as a way of communicating the will of the gods and predicting the future.

- **Dream Books** have been found dating back to the Old Kingdom. They list dreams such as breaking stones, losing teeth, having one's face turn into a leopard, drinking warm beer and drowning in the Nile.

- **The library of Scribe Kenherkhopeshef** contained a Dream Book papyrus. It contains the interpretations of over 100 dreams. Most deal with the dreamer's gains and losses, or physical events.

- **The interpretation of a dream** was often based on verbal connections. The Egyptian words for 'donkey' and 'great' were the same, so a dream about a donkey meant good luck.

- **Thutmose IV was told in a dream** that if he cleared away the sand from the feet of the Sphinx at Giza he would become king of Egypt.

- **Revelatory dreams** were thought to be very important. These were dreams that might show the dreamer the location of hidden treasure or a medicine to cure a sick patient. Doctors sometimes asked patients to look for cures in these sorts of dreams.

- **'Teachings for Merikare'**, written by King Kheti between 2070 and 2100 BC, took the opposite approach. It advised that dreams actually meant the opposite of what they appeared to be about.

- **It was also believed** that dreams allowed the living to see the activities of the deceased. People were also afraid of being exposed to malicious spirits while they were sleeping.

● **From the Late Period**, people began to sleep in temple complexes hoping that the intentions of the gods might be communicated to them through divinely inspired dreams.

● **Special priests** were appointed from the Late Period onward to interpret these dreams. These priests were known by the Greek term 'onirocrites'.

DREAM	MEANING
Bed catching fire	Breakdown of a marriage
Cat	Omen of a good crop
Deep well	Time in prison
Mirror	Second marriage
Shining moon	Forgiveness
Plunging into cold waters	Absolution of all ills
Crocodile meat	Good luck
Warm beer	Bad luck

Houses and gardens

- **According to the Greek historian** Diodorus Siculus, Egyptian dwellings were constructed of papyrus reeds until the 1st century BC.

- **More sophisticated houses** were built using sun-dried bricks. This technique has been used for nearly 6000 years. Mud from the Nile was mixed with chaff and shaped with frames before being baked in the sun.

▼ *Noblemen usually had large houses in extensive grounds, surrounded by high walls.*

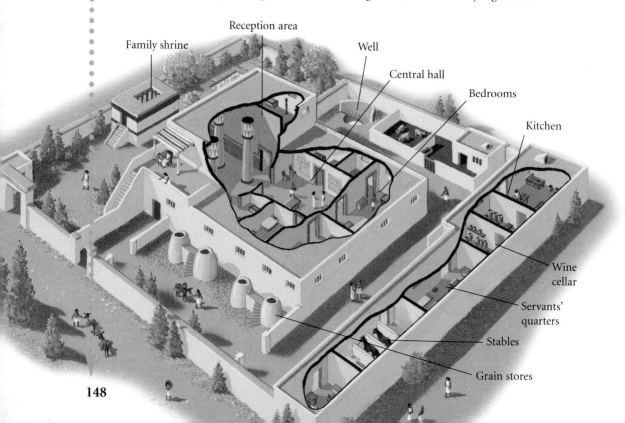

Family shrine

Reception area

Well

Central hall

Bedrooms

Kitchen

Wine cellar

Servants' quarters

Stables

Grain stores

...FASCINATING FACT...

...FASCINATING FACT...

Town houses stood two to three storeys high. The ground floor was usually reserved for businesses, while the upper floors provided family living space. Many people slept on their flat roofs in summer.

- **The rooms of larger houses** would have been arranged around an inner courtyard or on either side of a corridor. Windows would have been covered with shutters or blinds to keep out the dust, insects and constant heat.

- **A worker's house** had between two and four rooms at ground level, and an enclosed courtyard. There were two cellars for storage, and recesses in the walls for items such as household gods.

- **The houses of the rich** had several bedrooms, reception rooms and private quarters. Some may even have had bathrooms, toilets and swimming pools.

- **Water was drawn from wells** from the time of the New Kingdom. The water was raised with a shaduf (see page 10) into a pond.

- **Gardens were very popular**. Egyptian art shows gardens ranging from a few fruit trees to great botanical gardens with exotic trees and ponds, often stocked with fish, caged animals and birds.

- **Tomb paintings, engravings** and other pieces of art suggest that Egyptian gardens may have been very formal.

- **Gardeners were often employed** by wealthy Egyptians and in temples. They watered and weeded plants, and grew certain species from seed, including the date palm.

Hunting

- **The first people** to arrive in Egypt hunted wild animals to survive. These included ostriches, gazelles and giraffes. Scenes of these early chases are depicted in prehistoric cave art in Egypt.

- **Hippos were hunted** by men in papyrus boats armed with harpoons. This was because of the damage they did to crops.

- **Birds provided a rich source of food**, and were hunted and killed by hurling wooden throwsticks. Dogs and cats were trained to collect the birds struck down.

- **Small birds** were caught in nets. Large numbers of migrating species were caught when they landed after crossing the Mediterranean.

...FASCINATING FACT...

On a hunting expedition, the pharaoh rode out in his chariot accompanied by soldiers wearing full military dress. Amenhotep III once boasted of slaying 96 wild bulls during such a hunt.

- **Many examples of Egyptian wall art** depict birds being caught in nets. It was probably to illustrate the preservation of harmony, with the struggling birds in the nets representing the suppression of evil.

- **Fish were usually caught** in baskets made from willow branches, or with nets held between two boats. Bigger fish were tackled with spears. Fishing was also a way to relax and enjoy a day by the river.

- **Angling could be dangerous**. One species of catfish was armed with a poisonous spine. An Egyptian relief shows a man pulling one of these fish out of the catch and extracting the dangerous spine.

- **Wealthy Egyptians** may have been among the first people to have hunted for pleasure. They chased animals such as antelopes, foxes and hares for sport, together with the more dangerous wild bulls, elephants and lions.

- **Egyptian hunting scenes** often show kings tracking wild beasts inside enclosed grounds guarded by soldiers. These scenes have a hidden meaning. Wild creatures were associated with the wicked god Seth, so these pieces of art symbolized the pharaoh's triumph over evil.

▼ *The hippopotamus was viewed as an evil creature, because it often destroyed and ate crops. Hippo hunting was very important – if a king managed to kill a hippo, it was thought to symbolize the slaying of evil.*

Creation myths

- **Like many ancient cultures**, the Egyptians invented creation stories to explain how the world had come into existence.

- **One creation myth** suggested that the world had been made by a god called Ptah by the power of thought. He was depicted as a green-skinned mummy.

▼ *The Sun is linked with many of the Egyptian creation myths. The creator god Atum was a solar god, who was eventually renamed as the sun god Ra.*

- **Another story** puts forward the idea that the universe was originally a sea of chaos inside a god called Nun. One day, a mound of land rose out of this sea, and gradually formed the land of Egypt.

- **Nun was a god of chaos** and infinity, greatly feared by the ancient Egyptians. They believed that he might one day sink the world back into the ocean of chaos.

- **They also believed** that Nun was responsible for darkness, as every night he carried the sun god Ra away through the underworld until the next morning.

- **Ra was the god of the sun** and light. The Egyptians believed that a blue lotus flower appeared on the dark waters of Nun, and unfurled its petals to reveal Ra, who then created the world and everything in it.

- **The Egyptians did not understand** the way the Earth rotates around the sun and why the sun rises and sets every day. They believed the sun was rolled across the sky every day by the god Khepri.

- **Night and day** was explained by the story of the twin gods Nut and Keb. They hugged each other so tightly they blocked out the sun's rays, upsetting the sun god Ra.

- **To create daylight,** Ra ordered that the twins be separated and Nut was raised up to become the sky. Keb became the Earth. As night fell, the twins were reunited, as Nut came down to earth to be with her brother.

- **The Egyptians believed** that the sun god Ra was the first pharaoh. After Ra, they thought that all pharaohs came into the world as humans.

Dance

- **The ancient Egyptians loved to dance.** Pottery vessels dating from before the Pre-dynastic period have been found, decorated with dancers raising their arms above their heads.

- **Professional dancers** were usually women. Scenes suggest they wore skirts or loose tunics with shoulder straps. Sometimes they appeared covered in long shawls.

- **Many ancient wall paintings and carvings** depict scenes of Egyptians singing and dancing. It is difficult to tell exactly what the dance movements of the Egyptians were like, but the scenes show them clapping, hopping and skipping.

- **Dancers also performed acrobatics** including backbends, flips, cartwheels, high-kicks and handstands.

- **Archaeologists have yet to find** any depictions of men and women dancing together. The most common scenes show solo dancers, or groups of female dancers, usually performing in pairs.

- **During the Old Kingdom**, funeral rituals often included dance. Dance was an expression of mourning for the dead and a way of marking the regeneration of the body.

- **Other groups of dancers** followed the funerary procession to the tomb. The *mww*-dancers performed as the procession reached the tomb. Their dance symbolized the dead being led to the underworld.

- **Dance was a way of celebrating** the joy and revelry of feast days.

- **Dancing in temples** marked important festivals such as the jubilee ceremony, known as the Sed. This usually involved a solemn procession carrying a statue of the temple god.

▲ *Dancing was often combined with gymnastics and acrobatics in ancient Egypt.*

● **Dancing dwarfs** were a special attraction. The Egyptians believed that they never grew old because they never grew past the height of a child. Pepy II praised one of his officials for bringing back a dwarf for 'god's dances' from a southern expedition.

Music

- **Egyptian art suggests** that musicians were nearly always men in the Old Kingdom. By the time of the New Kingdom, they were mostly women.

- **There is no evidence** to suggest that the ancient Egyptian used any form of musical notation. Some ancient Egyptian instruments have survived, while many more are depicted on pottery and other artefacts dating back to the Pre-dynastic era.

- **A wide variety** of percussion instruments were played. Rhythms were beaten out on tambourines, ivory clappers, drums, castanets, cymbals and an array of chiming bells.

- **Stringed instruments** included the lyre (a form of lute) and the harp. These resemble versions that were introduced from Asia.

- **Wind instruments** included wooden pipes (similar to modern Egyptian folk clarinets) and early flutes, which were made from reeds and later, bronze. Bugle-like trumpets were used in religious ceremonies and in battle.

- **Festivals and holy days** were marked by music and singing. Groups of musicians would sometimes have to entertain thousands of people.

- **Such festivals were frequent**. One village in the Fayum region dedicated 150 days every year to feasting in the name of the gods.

...FASCINATING FACT...
Both men and women could be musicians in ancient Egypt, but there were some instruments that were played only by men, and some that were played only by women.

- **Music was also** a part of everyday life, providing a natural rhythm to workers' tasks. Farm labourers sang to their livestock, and sticks were clapped together as grapes were crushed at harvest time.

- **In Old and Middle Kingdom tombs**, inscriptions of songs and hymns were sung to the accompaniment of a harp to celebrate the dead.

▼ *Stringed instruments such as harps and lutes were often played during banquets in ancient Egypt.*

Sports

- **It was important** that young men were in good physical condition because it was always possible that they would have to go into the army. Kings, princes and statesmen usually supported sports competitions.

- **Early versions of many modern sports** were played to strict rules. Inscriptions reveal that a wide variety of sports were played, from wrestling and weightlifting, to a host of ball games.

▼ *Scenes of ancient Egyptians boxing for sport were found in the tomb of 'Mery Ra' and the 'Ptah Hotep' tomb in Saqqara.*

- **The ancient Egyptians invented** many aspects of sport that are still in use today. These included neutral referees, uniforms for players and awarding medals to winners.

- **The sport of handball**, depicted on the Saqqara tombs, was played by four women. Each had to throw the ball to the other at the same time. Players could be on their feet or on a teammate's back while exchanging balls.

- **The Saqqara tombs** depict boxing scenes. Two fighters stand fist to fist, dressed only in loincloths. Pharaohs and princes paid to watch.

- **Ball games were popular** among Egyptian boys. Balls made of leather skins filled with tightly-bound papyrus reeds were used in a number of hockey-type games.

- **Swimming was the most popular** competitive sport. The Nile was often used to practise in, but swimming pools were also built in palaces for the use of noblemen.

- **Long-distance running** was a most important sport in ancient Egypt. It had a religious significance when a new pharaoh was being crowned.

- **As part of the coronation**, the king ran a long distance around a temple before spectators, to show his physical strength and ability to rule using his might as well as his brain.

- **Archery was a popular sport**, and the practise of it was also important training for battle. Amenhotep II boasted that he pierced the middle of a thick brass target with four arrows. He offered a prize to anyone who could do the same.

Games and toys

- **Board games** were hugely popular in ancient Egypt. They were enjoyed by both adults and children. Board games and toys are among the oldest items found in Egypt.

- *Senet* **was a game** in which two players competed to be the first reach the kingdom of the gods. Each player had between five and seven pieces at one end of the papyrus board. The object of the game was to move all your pieces to the other end.

- **One of the oldest board games** was *Mehen*, or 'snake'. Players moved pieces around a spiral board until they reached the snake's head in the centre.

- **The game Hounds and Jackals** may be the forerunner of Snakes and Ladders. The oldest board found dates from the First Intermediate Period.

- **Toys were usually simple** and were fashioned out of wood, stone, ivory, ceramics or bone. Surviving examples range from skittles and dolls to whipping-tops and throwsticks.

- **Some of the toys** are fairly elaborate. The British Museum holds a model of a crocodile with a moving jaw. Toys with moving parts that could be made to spin by pulling strings have been found at el Lisht.

- **Children played against each other** for marbles. Their game seems to have been based on a miniature version of skittles.

> ....FASCINATING FACT....
> Archaeologists have discovered mysterious rows of holes bored into the roofs and floors of Egyptian temples. Some think that these were used for a board game called Wari, which is still played in Africa today.

160

▲ *Board games were a popular family pursuit. Children played with simple toys that were often home-made.*

- **Egyptian children played** games such as leapfrog, tug-of-war, arm-wrestling and juggling. Some of these are shown in paintings and carvings.

- **Many of the games** Egyptian children played may have been early versions of modern games such as Grandmother's Footsteps and Blind-man's Buff.

161

Ancient storytelling

- **Egyptian stories** were passed on verbally through generations. Some were written down on papyrus and *ostraca* – 'scraps of pottery'.

- **Stories were told for entertainment** but many also contained important, often moral, messages.

- **The earliest written story** dates from the Middle Kingdom and was composed in Middle Egyptian, the classical language of that period.

▼ *The legend of Osiris tells that he was the dead form of an earthly ruler who rose from the dead to become king of the gods.*

- **Ancient autobiographies** have been discovered, including the life story of the official Weni, who served from the reign of King Teti to that of King Merenre. In it, Weni greatly exaggerates his position in court.

- **One of the oldest stories** was the tale of the courtier Sinuhe, preserved in six papyri and two dozen *ostraca*. It tells of his flight from Egypt after the death of King Amenemhat. After many years, Sinuhe writes a letter begging for forgiveness from King Senusret I, who allows Sinuhe to return and be reinstated at the royal court.

- **The story of Sinuhe** was popular with all levels of society. The supervisor of the tomb builders in the Valley of the Kings requested that a copy of the book should be placed in his tomb for him to take to the afterlife.

- **The mythical tale** *The Book of the Cow of Heaven* described how the sun god Ra sent Hathor to quash a rebellion by mankind. She developed a taste for killing and refused to return, so Ra created a beer that looked like human blood. Hathor drank it and became intoxicated.

- **In the story of Setne Khamwas**, a son of Ramesses II encounters the ghost of a long dead magician in his tomb at Saqqara.

- **In the** *Tale of the Unlucky Prince*, the Seven Hathors predict that a baby prince will die because he will be attacked by a crocodile, a snake or a dog. A beautiful princess saves him from the snake. Unfortunately, the end of the papyrus is missing, so we do not know how the story ends.

- **Travel stories** that featured magic were popular. *The Tale of the Shipwrecked Sailor* begins with a sailor stranded on a magic island after a storm. A giant serpent rescues him before the island mysteriously sinks beneath the waves.

Zoos, parks and exotic gardens

- **The keeping of animals** for pleasure was common in ancient Egypt. Zoos were popular, and many kept dangerous wild animals.

- **Exotic animals** such as elephants, bears, giraffes and ostriches usually entered Egypt in official trading expeditions, or as tribute (tax) that Nubia and other parts of the empire had to pay to Egypt.

- **The earliest-known captive polar bear** was owned by Ptolemy II at his private zoo at Alexandria.

- **Queen Hatshepsut** was very interested in wild beasts. She kept a number of baboons, which she was given when she had myrrh saplings brought from the Horn of Africa.

- **Pharaoh Akhenaten** kept wild animals and a bird aviary at his northern palace at the city of Akhetaten.

- **Animals were sometimes treated very poorly**. The story *Lion in Search of Man* details a horrific practice given out to a bear whose claws and teeth were removed.

> ...FASCINATING FACT...
> During the 5th Dynasty, Syrian bears were brought to Egypt. They were kept on leashes in the homes of the wealthy, who seemed to have little regard for their own safety.

164

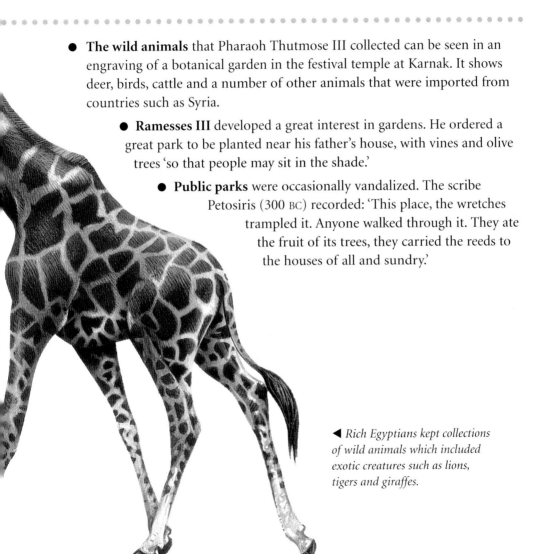

- **The wild animals** that Pharaoh Thutmose III collected can be seen in an engraving of a botanical garden in the festival temple at Karnak. It shows deer, birds, cattle and a number of other animals that were imported from countries such as Syria.

  - **Ramesses III** developed a great interest in gardens. He ordered a great park to be planted near his father's house, with vines and olive trees 'so that people may sit in the shade.'

    - **Public parks** were occasionally vandalized. The scribe Petosiris (300 BC) recorded: 'This place, the wretches trampled it. Anyone walked through it. They ate the fruit of its trees, they carried the reeds to the houses of all and sundry.'

◀ *Rich Egyptians kept collections of wild animals which included exotic creatures such as lions, tigers and giraffes.*

165

Festivals

- **Hundreds of festivals** were celebrated by the people of the kingdom. Calendars on temple walls, studded with special markers, reveal that some temples marked dozens of religious holidays a year.

- **In the festival hall** of Thutmose III at Karnak, a list details the 54 feast days that were celebrated every year. Sixty festivals were celebrated every year at the mortuary temple of Ramesses III.

- **Many of these festivals** involved carrying an image of the god from one temple to another. This allowed ordinary Egyptians a glimpse of the image, which would normally be hidden away inside the temple.

- **The Festival of Opet** was celebrated from the early 18th Dynasty onwards in the second month of the season of the *akhet* (flood) season. The main event was the procession that carried divine images from Karnak to Luxor.

- **The Festival of the Valley** took place at Thebes from the 18th Dynasty onwards. The statues of Amun, Mut and Khons were carried from Karnak to Deir El-Bahri on the opposite side of the Nile.

- **The festival of the fertility god** Min was celebrated during the first month of the *shemu* (harvesting) season. The statue of the god was carried out of his temple and placed on a platform in the country. During the reign of Ramesses III the pharaoh himself walked at the front of the procession.

- **A festival was held** to mark the murder of Osiris. His tragic story was performed, and the whole country went into mourning. After several days, priests announced that he had risen from the dead, and only then were people were allowed to celebrate.

- **Divine images** were usually carried by priests in special gilded boats that were fixed to the top of poles.

FESTIVAL	SIGNIFICANCE	CELEBRATION
New Year's Day (Wep-renpet)	Celebrate rejuvenation and re-birth	Feasting
Feast of Wagy	Celebration of the god Thoth	Two feasts
Opet	To honour the God Amun	Procession and ceremony in the temple of Amun
The Beautiful Feast of the Valley	To honour the dead	Offerings are made to the dead
Heb-Sed	To prove that the pharaoh is still fit to rule after 30 years as pharaoh	Ceremony in which the pharaoh must prove himself fit and capable

- **On festival days**, temple altars were piled high with food and drink. For the poor, these events represented a rare opportunity to taste delicacies such as wine and roast beef.
- **The quantity of food consumed** during festivals was staggering. During the Opet festival more than 11,000 loaves and cakes were eaten, and 385 measures of beer were consumed. At the Sokar festival, more than 7400 loaves were eaten and nearly 1500 measures of beer were drunk.

Scribes

▲ *The ancient Egyptians believed that hieroglyphic writing came from Thoth.*

● **The term scribe** is a translation of the Egyptian word *sesh*, meaning the government officials and administrators of the Egyptian kingdom. Scribes were civil servants.

● **Scribes wrote diplomatic letters**, calculated and collected taxes, took notes during court cases, organized building projects, and copied out religious texts.

● **Positions as scribes** were highly coveted and the profession became hereditary. One scribe, Horemheb, became so powerful he went on to become pharaoh.

● **The scribe** was often depicted with legs crossed, and his papyrus across his lap.

● **Evidence of a school for scribes** has been found at Deir el-Medina. Training began with the students copying passages from the *Book of Kemyt*. They then progressed to copying works of literature.

● **A scribe's kit** consisted of a rectangular basalt palette with two holes in it, into which cakes of ink could be inserted. There was also space for reed pens, a water pot, and a knife for trimming papyrus sheets. A stone was carried to smooth the surface of the paper.

● **Thoth was the god of the scribes.** He was depicted as a man with the head of an ibis bird, and carried a pen and scrolls. Scribes prayed to him for success in their work.

- **The profession of scribe** was privileged. Part of a text giving advice to a schoolboy reads: 'Be a scribe! It saves you from labour and protects you from all kinds of work. It spares you from using the hoe and the mattock... the scribe, he directs all the work in this land!'

- **One of Egypt's most famous scribes** was a man called Ahmas (1680–1620 BC). One of his best-known writings was the text 'Accurate reckoning, the entrance into the knowledge of all existing things and all obscure secrets'.

- **The scribe Imhotep** lived 4500 years ago. He was a high priest and also designed the world's first pyramid at Saqqara. After his death, the ancient Egyptians came to see him as a god.

▼ *Writing materials used by scribes included papyrus, reed pens, and pots that were used to hold ink.*

Hieroglyphics

- **Hieroglyphics is a form** of writing using pictures and symbols. There were about 700 symbols in the system, which was first used in the 4th millennium BC.

- **The word 'hieroglyph' is Greek**, meaning 'sacred carving'. The ancient Egyptians called their writing 'the divine words'.

- **Hieroglyphics was often written** on a form of paper called papyrus. It was named after the plant from which it was made, and was first manufactured around 3100 BC.

▲ *Hieroglyphs were painted or carved into walls. Many are still visible in tombs.*

- **Hieroglyph symbol images** were usually pictures from the natural world of Egypt. The letter 'M', for example, was represented by the barn owl, while other signs included images of quail chicks and loaves of bread.

- **Some hieroglyphs represent sounds**, while others stand for ideas. One symbol showed the sound of a word, followed by another symbol to explain what type of word it was. Vowel sounds were not written down.

- **Hieroglyphics could be written** from left to right, right to left or from top to bottom. If the symbols for animals or people faced left, they were read from left to right. If they faced right, they were read from right to left.

- **Hieratic was a simplified form** of hieroglyphics. This script was used for business transactions and religious documents. It was usually written on papyrus or pieces of stone or pottery called *ostraca*.

- **In the first millennium** BC a script called *demotic* began to replace hieratic. Demotic means 'popular script'. This was followed in the 1st century BC by a form called Coptic Script.

- **Coptic Script** contained the 24 letters of the Greek alphabet and six signs from the demotic script. Vowel sounds were written down for the first time. Knowledge of this script proved crucial in deciphering the Rosetta Stone (see page 192).

- **By the 6th century** AD, when the last Egyptian temple was closed after the fall of the Roman Empire, the art of reading hieroglyphs was lost until 1799.

◀ *Hieroglyphic symbols were essentially diagrams of the object or idea the artist was trying to convey by writing.*

171

Art

- **The first pieces of Egyptian art** were scratched onto cave walls around 5000 BC. They show the type of animals that were hunted for food. It is thought the Egyptians believed that painting these creatures would give the artist the power to capture them.

- **In the age of the pharaohs**, artists were commissioned to paint pictures of important Egyptians after they had died, so that their memory could live on. Many nobles, officials and their families were painted after their deaths.

- **Artists were usually male** and learned their craft when they were young. At the beginning of their training they were given tasks such as mixing colours, fetching water and making brushes, before progressing to making sketches on rocks, stones and scraps of papyrus.

- **The colours** that artists used were brilliantly vibrant, and have lasted remarkably well over thousands of years. Different minerals were used to make different colours – carbon for black, ochre for red and yellow, and azurite and malachite for green and blue.

- **Teams of master artists** worked on large wall paintings. They were planned on a board marked with grids. The wall was then marked with a scaled-up grid, and the painting was copied onto the wall at the enlarged size.

- **In Egyptian art**, figures are not usually depicted face on. A person's head is usually turned right or left. The eye is always shown in full frontal view.

- **As a result of this style**, paintings of figures were not very realistic, because a single portrait included a variety of viewpoints.

- **Paintings usually adopted a hierarchal scale.** If the king was featured, he would be shown much larger than his servants who were ranked in size according to their importance.

- **Some of the best-preserved paintings** are murals in the rooms that lead to tombs. The paintings and their accompanying hieroglyphics describe stories about the pharaoh's journey into the afterlife.

- **Ancient Egyptians made a distinction** between draughtsmen and painters. Draughtsmen were called *sesh kedut* – 'writers of outlines'.

▼ *Egyptian artists painted pharaohs, possessions, food and other items that the deceased might need in the afterlife on tomb walls.*

Mathematics

- **The Greeks are usually credited** with inventing mathematics. However, the oldest recorded evidence for the use of mathematics was found in ancient Egypt and dated back to around 2000 BC.

- **Reading and writing numbers** in ancient Egypt was relatively simple. It used a system of symbols. The higher number was always written in front of the lower number.

- **There was no sign for zero** in the Egyptian numerical system. Scribes sometimes left a gap between numbers where a zero should be.

- **The Egyptian decimal system** had seven different symbols.

- **Our knowledge of Egyptian mathematics** is based on a tiny number of texts. The only evidence found so far comes from four papyri, a leather scroll and two wooden tablets.

- **The Rhind Mathematical Papyrus**, found in a tomb in Thebes, is packed full of fractions and complex calculations relating to the volumes of triangles, rectangles and pyramids.

- **Despite the dry mathematical nature of the text,** the last problem posed in the Rhind Mathematical Papyrus may be an Egyptian joke. It asks how much corn might be saved if 343 mice were eaten by 49 cats in seven houses!

- **The Egyptians used mathematics** in calculating how to set out the great pyramids. By working out the area of a circle according to the length of its diameter they could calculate the volume of a pyramid.

- **The ancient Egyptians** had no abstract formulae like the Greeks. Instead, they tackled mathematical problems by a series of smaller calculations.

MATHEMATICAL SYMBOLS

1 was shown by a single stroke.

10 was represented by a hobble for cattle.

100 was represented by a coil of rope.

1000 was represented by a lotus plant.

10,000 was represented by a finger.

100,000 was represented by a tadpole or frog.

1,000,000 was represented by a figure of a god with arms raised.

● **Scribes learned mathematics** by copying set examples and replacing figures with their own answers. Archaeologists have discovered ancient exercise sheets, with teacher's markings on them.

Craftwork

- **The ancient Egyptians** were extremely skilful carpenters. They could fashion tables, chairs and boxes with joints similar to those in use today.

- **Very little timber** was readily available in Egypt. Apart from a few acacia trees, tamarisk and willow, most of the wood was imported from Lebanon.

- **An adze** was used for carving and planing. It had a wooden handle and a blade fitted at the top. Early forms of drills were rotated by an implement like an archer's bow.

- **Carpentry was a demanding trade**. The excerpt below from a scribe reveals just how arduous this type of work could be: 'Every carpenter who picks up the adze is more tired than a peasant... There is no end to his labour. He has to work more than his arms are capable of.'

- **The tomb of Rekhmire at Thebes** contains a series of pictures of carpenters. These sketches reveal the wide array of tools they used to ply their trade.

- **A carpenter worked on rough wood** with an axe. Logs were split, and then chopped into smaller chunks. A saw was then used to slice into the wood.

- **Carpenters used a vice** to hold pieces of wood when sawing. The piece of timber was tied to a pole that was rammed into the ground, possibly with a weight attached to one end to keep the rope taut.

- **Bones were ground** to make a natural glue. An early form of plaster was also used. Gesso was made by mixing whiting with glue. It was harder than plaster, stuck better to wood and was an excellent base for painting.

> **...FASCINATING FACT...**
> Rulers were used to check that lines and edges were straight, and
> set squares were used to make right angles.

● **Stones were used** to scour wood to ensure there were no rough edges, a practice that continued on ships (holystoning) until the 19th century.

◄ *Craftworkers were responsible for designing the great buildings and monuments of the Pharaonic era. They also created the tools that were needed to fashion wood, stone and precious metals.*

177

Making fine things

- **Egyptian jewellers** made objects such as amulets, rings, necklaces and girdles using gold, silver and semi-precious stones.

- **By the Middle Kingdom**, gold was the most precious material in Egypt. The first ever geological map is a diagram of gold mines and quarries in the Wadi Hammamat.

- **The process of casting** was used to make many metal objects. Metal was heated until it became liquid and then poured into moulds.

- **The ancient Egyptians exploited the mines** between the Nile and the Red Sea coast. Gold was mined from both the Eastern Desert and from Nubia, where Egyptian inscriptions date back to 3100 BC.

- **In Nubia**, workers used two methods for extracting gold. Rocks were smashed and the lumps of gold ore removed. More gold was washed out and caught in a sieve – possibly made out of a sheep fleece.

▶ *Most gold arrived in Egypt from Nubia. When it arrived it was weighed before being sent to workshops where goldsmiths made it into statues, jewellery and other beautiful objects.*

- **The technique of welding** was used by jewellers from the Middle Kingdom onwards. Different metals were heated until they became workable. The whole artefact was then joined over a ceramic furnace and a blowpipe used to increase the heat until the two pieces were welded together.

- **The technique of soldering** was in use from the 4th Dynasty onwards. Hard-soldering was preferred to soft-soldering as the artefact could be reheated without the bond melting.

- **The best example** of the goldsmiths' art are the funeral masks of pharaohs. Tutankhamun's beautiful death mask is a wonderful testament to their skill and ingenuity.

- **The first glass beads** were made in Pre-dynastic times. In the Old and Middle Kingdoms, artists made glass amulets, animal figures and other items. In the reign of Tuthmosis I in the New Kingdom, the first glass vessels were made.

- **Most of the pottery** was made from reddish-brown clay, and is called Nile silt ware. It was not highly valued and was left without decoration.

Around the home

- **The Egyptians furnished their houses simply**. The survival of objects in tombs and the illustration of furniture in art has allowed historians to gain a better understanding of how furniture was used in the home than perhaps in any other ancient civilization.

- **A famous example** of an Egyptian chair was recovered from the tomb of Tutankhamun. Chairs made for use in the home were made of carved wood, and were covered with leather or cloth. They were much lower than modern chairs.

- **Low stools** were used in most homes. By the time of the Middle Kingdom, folding stools were in use. A folding stool with legs that end in carved duck heads has been recovered from the tomb of Tutankhamun.

- **Most Egyptian families** did not have much in the way of spare possessions, but baskets were used to store items when they were not in use. These had the advantage of being cheap and easy to make and were light to carry around.

◄ *Representations of the dwarf god Bes were kept in many Egyptian homes because he was linked with protection of the family, fertility and childbirth.*

> **...FASCINATING FACT...**
> Beds with wooden frames have been traced back to the early dynastic period. Headrests were made of stone, ivory or wood.

- **Dining and gaming tables** were round, and mostly made of wood, though some stone and metal tables have been discovered.

- **In wealthier households**, boxes made from wood or ivory replaced baskets.

- **Jewellery and other valuables** were kept in storage chests, which were often highly decorated and fashioned out of materials such as alabaster.

- **Drawers were rare in ancient Egypt**, but they were sometimes built into certain pieces of furniture. Gaming tables often had drawers in which to store the counters.

- **Lamps were used** in the long winter evenings. Made out of pottery, they were filled with oils such as kiki oil and olive oil, and had floating wicks.

- **Wealthy Eygptians had limestone toilets**. Poorer families made do with toilet stools, under which stood a ceramic bowl.

▲ *Elaborate lamp stands held simple pottery bowls filled with oil and a wick.*

Astronomy and astrology

- **The ancient Egyptians** divided the night sky into 36 groups of star gods or constellations called decons. Each rose above the horizon every morning for ten days every year. The most important decon to the Egyptians was the dog star Sirius, the brightest star in the sky, which they believed that was the goddess Sopdet.

- **From the Old Kingdom onwards,** the Egyptians believed that humans could be reborn in the form of stars. Many pieces of tomb art from this era show vast numbers of stars to reflect this belief.

- **In ancient writings** called the Pyramid Texts, the author asks for the sky goddess Nut to place him 'among the imperishable stars.'

- **Astronomy was used** to predict the changes of the seasons. The Egyptians noted the times when Sirius rose with the Sun. This was called the 'Sothic rising', and it indicated that the flood season would soon arrive.

- **The ceremony of Pedj Shes** (Stretching the Cord) dates back to 2686 BC. It was performed to determine precisely the correct alignment for the building of foundations of the pyramids and sun temples. It relied on sightings of Orion and the Great Bear constellations, using a sighting tool made of a palm leaf.

- **The 'Sothic rising' of Sirius** coincided with the beginning of the solar year (the number of days it takes for the Earth to orbit the Sun) only once every 1460–1456 years. It happened in 2781–2777 BC, 1321–1317 BC and in AD 139 during the reign of the Roman emperor Antonius Pius. A coin was minted at Alexandria to commemorate the event. The period between these risings is known as the 'Sothic Cycle'.

- **The earliest evidence of true astronomical knowledge** in Egypt are diagonal calendars or star clocks. These have been found painted on the coffin lids of early Middle Kingdom and Late Period.

- **By the Middle Kingdom** the Egyptians had identified five of the planets: Jupiter ('Horus who limits two lands'), Mars ('Horus of the horizon', or 'Horus the red'), Mercury (Sebegu, a god associated with Seth), Saturn ('Horus, bull of the sky') and Venus ('the one who crosses', or 'god of the morning'). They believed the planets were gods that sailed across the heavens in boats called barques.

- **The first appearance of the zodiac** we know today was during the Ptolemaic period. It was painted on the ceiling of the chapel of Osiris on the roof of the temple of Hathor at Dendera in the 1st century AD.

...FASCINATING FACT...
Egyptian calendars had a major flaw. The Egyptian year was approximately six hours short, so that every 40 years, 10 days went missing!

Early travellers

- **Around 450 BC,** the Greek historian Herodotus visited ancient Egypt and recorded in detail the traditions and beliefs of its people. He was followed by Diodorus Siculus in 57 BC, and the Roman geographer Strabo, who journeyed up the Nile in 30 BC and wrote about the trip in his book *Geographica*.

- **In the 1st century** AD, a Greek priest and philosopher called Plutarch also studied ancient religious beliefs in Egypt. His book *De Iside et Osiride* examines the Egyptian people's worship of Isis and Osiris.

- **The next account of the region** was not written until the late 16th century. In 1589 an unknown merchant referred to as the Anonymous Venetian penned an account of a journey to Upper Egypt.

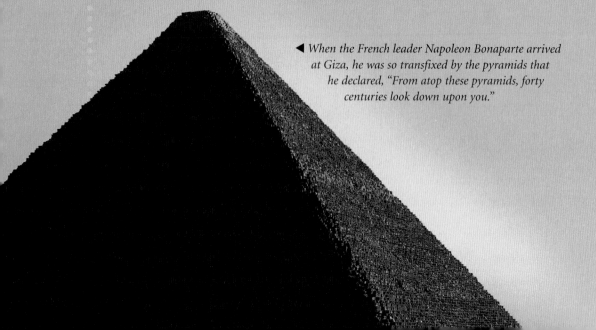

◀ *When the French leader Napoleon Bonaparte arrived at Giza, he was so transfixed by the pyramids that he declared, "From atop these pyramids, forty centuries look down upon you."*

- **The first accurate measurements** of the pyramids were taken in 1638 by an English astronomer called John Graves. He visited Giza and wrote *Pyrmaidographia*.

- **Claude Sicard** was a French priest who drew the first accurate map of Egypt. It pinpointed the major monuments, and where he thought the ancient cities were located.

- **The first great archaeological discovery** was made in 1768 by English traveller James Bruce, who discovered the tomb of Ramesses III in the Valley of the Kings. In 1798 Napoleon Bonaparte invaded Egypt, taking with him 40 scientists to record ancient and modern life along the Nile. Their findings were published in 1809 in a book called *Description de l'Egypte*.

- **The temple of Abu Simbel** was discovered in 1813. By 1818 it had been entered by Italian explorer Giovanni Battista Belzoni. He also located the tomb of Sethos I, and the entrance to the pyramid of Chephren.

- **Auguste Mariette** was a French archaeologist who established the Egyptian Antiquities Service and the Egyptian Museum of Cairo in 1858. Among his greatest discoveries were the catacomb of the sacred Apis bulls at Saqqara, and the Valley Temple of the pyramid of Chephren at Giza.

- **Mariette's work** was continued by Gaston Maspero. His work in tracking down tomb robbers led him to where priests of the 21st Dynasty had hidden the mummies of the most important pharaohs, including Amenophis I, Sethos I and Ramesses II.

- **British archaeological involvement in Egypt** accelerated in 1880 with the arrival of Egyptologist William Flinders Petrie. His important excavations included the Pre-dynastic necropolis of Naqada.

David Roberts

- **David Roberts (1796–1864) was born** near Edinburgh, Scotland. He was a talented artist as a child, and became an apprentice to a house painter.

- **He later worked** for a travelling circus painting scenary, but his true skills lay as an illustrator.

- **Roberts began to establish a reputation,** and forged friendships with creative minds of the day, including Charles Dickens and the artist J M W Turner. The writer John Wilkie persuaded Roberts that he should travel abroad to broaden his experiences.

- **The artist started to attract** wealthy patrons such as Lord Northwick, for whom he completed the *Departure of the Israelites* in 1829.

- **When Roberts painted this work**, he had never visited the Middle East. He worked from detailed descriptions and sketches that had been brought back by travellers.

- **In 1838, Roberts had earned** enough money to tour the monuments of ancient Egypt. He arrived in Alexandria on 24 September. A boat took him to Cairo, where he sketched the pyramids and Sphinx.

- **Roberts' journey** down the Nile took him as far as Abu Simbel. On the journey he sketched the monuments and landscape. Upon returning to Cairo, he stayed for a short while to work on his sketches.

- **Belgian engraver Louis Haghe then produced** 247 lithographs from Roberts' drawings. They were published in six volumes by Francis Graham Moon between 1842 and 1849.

- **In 1839 he undertook** the second part of his journey, in the company of two friends, travelling from Cairo through Suez, Sinai and Petra, the Holy Land and into modern-day Lebanon. He returned home after eleven months.

186

...FASCINATING FACT...

Roberts was amazed by the Nile. He described it as 'wending its way like a long winding sheet spangled with silver tears.'

▼ Books of David Roberts' sketches gave most people outside Egypt their first glimpse of what the pyramids and the Sphinx really looked like.

William Flinders Petrie

- **William Matthew Flinders Petrie** was the grandson of the first man to map Australia. His father, an engineer, taught him the art of map making.

- **By the age of 22** Petrie had written a book on ancient measurements used in prehistoric Britain, based on work he had done at Stonehenge.

- **Petrie's interest in Egypt** was fostered by books written by Charles Piazzi-Smyth, the Scottish Astronomer Royal, on the Great Pyramid of Giza.

- **Petrie went to Egypt** between 1880 and 1882 to test the mathematical measurements in Piazzi-Smyth's book. He journeyed to Giza and the Great Pyramids, Dahshur, the Bent Pyramid, Saqqara and Abu Rawash. Petrie also walked through the Theban tombs behind the temple of Medinet Habu.

- **Petrie eventually discovered** that every measurement Piazzi-Smyth had taken was inaccurate. His own survey, the *Pyramids and Temples of Giza*, was published in 1883. It remains a standard in Egyptology.

- **In 1884, Petrie was appointed** successor to Edouard Naville by the Egypt Exploration Fund. He was scathing of the unprofessional work carried out by his predecessors, and resigned in 1886.

- **Petrie established** what later became the British School of Archaeology in Egypt. He was also appointed the first Edwards Professor of Egyptology at University College in London, holding the post between 1892 and 1933.

...**FASCINATING FACT**...
Petrie earned the Arabic nickname 'Abu Bagousheh' – father of pots. On every trip to Egypt, he brought back heavily notated samples of pottery.

- **Petrie's greatest contribution** to Egyptology was the discovery of a long period of civilization before the 1st Dynasty – the Pre-dynastic Period. Extensive digs were carried out at sites around Naqada on the West Bank of the Nile 30 km north of Luxor.

- **Petrie was supported financially** by the writer Amelia Edwards. She was the founder of the Egypt Exploration Fund, and also set up a chair in Egyptology at University College London for Petrie.

▼ *After travelling to Egypt, Petrie wrote a book called* The Pyramids and Temples of Giza, *published in 1883. It is still a respected piece of work even today.*

Carter's discovery

- **One of the most dramatic** archaeological discoveries of all time was made in November 1922, when the English archaeologist Howard Carter discovered the virtually untouched tomb of the pharaoh Tutankhamun.

- **Carter was born in England** in 1874, and worked as an assistant to the archaeologist William Flinders Petrie. He was offered the job of Inspector of General of Monuments in Upper Egypt, based in Luxor, in 1899.

- **In 1905, Carter resigned** from the position. In 1907 he met English aristocrat Lord Carnarvon, who had a passion for archaeology. Carnarvon persuaded Carter to work for him, and Carter carried out a number of excavations on behalf of his employer.

- **Carter and Carnarvon** were granted a licence from the Egyptian Antiquities Service to dig in the Valley of the Kings in 1914. Carter was certain that the tomb of a young pharaoh called Tutankhamun was still buried somewhere in the valley.

- **Carter based his evidence** on a series of archaeological clues. Tutankhamun's name was inscribed on a stela (a carved stone pillar) at the temple of Karnak, and was also found on artefacts found in the Valley of the Kings by the American archaeologist Theodore Davis.

- **World War I delayed work** on the site until 1917. Progress was slow, and by 1921 very little had been found. Lord Carnarvon began to grow uneasy about the amount of money that the project was costing.

- **Carter was given one more year** to dig, beginning in autumn 1922. On 4 November, workmen found a stone step. This proved to be the first of an underground staircase.

► Carter and one of his team unbrick a wall leading into a passageway and eventually Tutankhamun's treasury. What they found inside remains probably the most spectacular discovery in archaeological history.

- **Excavation work began** on the site. The stairway was cleared, revealing a door, then a second, inner door, which had the name of a pharaoh on it – Tutankhamun.

- **On 26 November**, Carter and his team pierced a hole through the second door. The tomb inside was intact, and was full of some of the most spectacular treasures of ancient Egypt.

- **Emptying the tomb** took nearly a decade. About 3500 items were slowly catalogued and removed, including the fantastic coffin and mummy of the pharaoh.

191

The Rosetta Stone

- **The Rosetta Stone** is a piece of granite rock covered with ancient writing. Although it is fairly unimpressive to look at, it held the key to the secrets of ancient Egypt.

- **The stela was inscribed** in 196 BC with a decree issued at the city of Memphis. It was discovered in a small village in the Delta called Rosetta (el-Rashid).

- **Egyptologists were excited** about the stone because its inscription was written in three different languages – hieroglyphic, demotic and Greek. Because ancient Greek was understood, this meant theoretically it should be possible to decipher the text by comparing the languages.

- **The Rosetta Stone** was found by Napoleon's team of scientists in 1799. The French leader ordered plaster casts to be sent to scientists throughout Europe in the hope that somebody might be able to decipher the inscription.

- **When Napoleon** was defeated by the British, the Rosetta Stone was taken to the British Museum. There, European experts realized that the royal names they could understand in the Greek script were the same names that were enclosed in ovals (cartouches) in the hieroglyphic script.

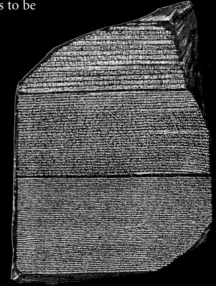

▶ *The Rosetta Stone is engraved with hieroglyphics at the top, followed by demotic script and finally Greek script at the bottom.*

- **An Egyptologist** called Thomas Young was responsible for deciphering the demotic text. He was able to decipher the names of Ptolemy and Cleopatra.

- **Hieroglyphic code** was cracked by a young French scholar called Jean Francois Champollion. In 1822, he worked out that hieroglyphics were actually a phonetic rather than a purely picture-based script.

- **Champollion published** the book *Lettre a M. Dacier* to announce his discovery to an incredulous world in 1822. Two years later, he wrote another book setting out the concepts of hieroglyphic writing.

- **We now know** that the Rosetta Stone was written by a group of priests to honour the pharaoh. The script praises the good things he had done for the people of Egypt.

...FASCINATING FACT...
Champollion visited Egypt in 1828. As the first scientist who could read the inscriptions on ancient Égyptian temples and tomb walls, he was treated with great reverence.

The temples of Abu Simbel

- **The temples of Abu Simbel** lie on the west bank of the Nile, about 850 km from Cairo. They were carved into a cliff face on the orders of the pharaoh Ramesses II, who was renowned for his huge building projects.

- **The larger temple** was dedicated to Ramesses II. Outside it stand four colossal statues of the king. The smaller temple, for his favourite wife Nefertari, is dedicated to Hathor. At the front are statues of the royal family.

- **Abu Simbel was left alone** by the civilizations that conquered Egypt, and left undisturbed until the beginning of the 19th century.

- **The temples** were rediscovered by Jean-Louise Burckhardt in 1813. The facade of the main temple was half buried in the desert sand, and he was unable to clear it.

- **The temples were a popular attraction** in the 19th century, even when covered in sand. Wealthy Europeans, particularly from Britain, flocked to the site.

- **The English explorer William Bankes** and his Italian servant Giovanni Finati visited the site in October 1815. They managed to enter Nefertari's temple, but the sand had covered everything except one of the four great statues outside the main temple.

- **A further unsuccessful attempt** to enter the great temple followed in 1816, led by French consul Bernardino Drovetti.

- **The man who eventually gained entry** to the temple was Italian Giovanni Belzoni. In 1803 he was employed by the British Consul General Henry Salt to search for treasures in ancient Egypt for the British Museum.

- **On 1 August 1817** Belzoni succeeded in clearing the 30 feet of sand that blocked the entrance to the main temple. He became the first person to step inside the temple for hundreds of years.

- **Belzoni was probably disappointed** when he saw that the temple was virtually empty, but the walls were carved with fabulous reliefs that illustrated the military campaigns of Ramesses II.

▼ *The largest temple at Abu Simbel is dedicated to three gods and Ramesses II, who was himself deified. Four gigantic statues of the pharaoh sit outside the entrance.*

Recent discoveries

- **A discovery was made** by the young architect Kamal el-Mallakh in the 1950s, while he was carrying out work on the pyramid of Khufu.

- **He discovered** the planking of a great ship. It had been dismantled and placed there over 4000 years ago in 13 layers and 1224 pieces.

- **The Egyptian Antiquities Organization** took 16 years to rebuild the ship. It is 43 m long, and nearly 6 m wide.

- **Optical equipment** produced evidence in 1985 to suggest that there is a second ship, perfectly preserved, buried beside the pyramid of Cheops.

- **An investigation** into the stability of the columns that supported the courtyard of Amenophis III in the Luxor temple led to a discovery in 1989.

- **Twenty statues were found** on the western side, mostly dating from the time of Amenophis III. These statues were given the name 'The Statues of Luxor'.

- **Another discovery** was made in 1989 in Akhmim. An 8-m-tall statue of Princess Meritamun, daughter of Ramesses II and Nefertari, was found.

- **Michel Redde**, director of the Institut Francais d'Archeologie Orientale of Cairo, found treasure that had once belonged to a high priest of the god Serapis in the oasis of Dush in March 1989.

- **In 1991, archaeologists at Giza** discovered the village where the labourers who built the Great Pyramid would have lived.

- **A Swiss/French mission** in April 2002 discovered a pyramid at the site of Abu Rowash dated to the reign of Djedefre.

▶ *Modern forensic techniques have allowed scientists to rebuild the face of the pharaoh Tutankhamun, based on his mummy.*

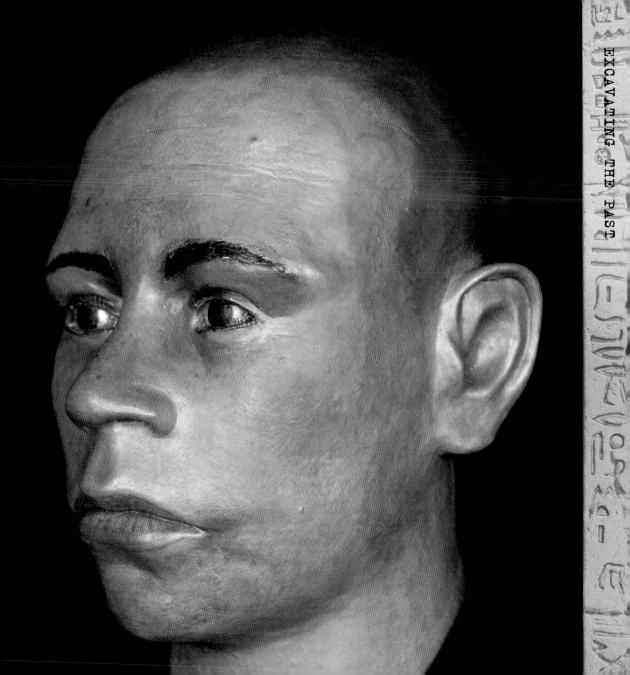

Rescue and salvage archaeology

- **Rescue archaeology** involves carrying out urgent excavations against the clock. These usually occur in areas where developers are waiting to move in, or if environmental changes are threatening an important site.

- **The most famous example** of rescue archaeology in action began on 6 April 1959, when the Egyptian government issued an appeal to UNESCO because the temples of Abu Simbel were in danger of being flooded as a dam was built.

- **Each temple was rebuilt** in exactly the same state as they had been in – broken statues were not repaired. As the temples were originally carved out of a sandstone cliff, an artificial mountain was created.

- **A museum was built** at Abu Simbel to house all the finds unearthed during the building work. Over 3000 artefacts were found, including four mummies of Egyptian nobles.

- **In the modern city** of Alexandria the rescue archaeologist Jean-Yves Empereur has started to look for traces of the Tower of Pharos. He has already salvaged some pieces of the Tower at the foot of Qaitbay Fort and hopes to find more.

> **...FASCINATING FACT...**
> When the temples of Abu Simbel were threatened by the Nile waters, they were cut out of the rock, lifted above the floodplain, and rebuilt in a safe location.

- **The remains** of the city of Pharaoh Akhenaten are little more than rubble at present. A British company called Akhenaten City PLC, is trying to reconstruct the central area of the city. The city is situated on Luxor's west bank and it is hoped that it will be a major tourist attraction.

- **In Luxor's Avenue of the Sphinxes**, some of Egypt's most treasured sandstone structures are literally turning to dust. Engineers from the University of Missouri-Rolla are investigating a remedy.

- **In November 2002**, UNESCO began assessing water damage at Luxor Temple and monuments at Abu Mena.

- **Plans to construct** a massive canal across Egypt's northern Sinai Desert would affect several valuable archaeological sites. In 1991 the North Sinai Salvage Project was launched to survey the canal's path and suggest a possible alternative route.

▲ *The Tower of Pharos was built in the Ptolemaic period, and it is likely that it was the first lighthouse ever built. Archaeologists have found the foundations, but are searching for remnants of the structure today.*

- **In 2000**, government officials in Egypt called for a major salvage operation to protect the ancient monuments of the northern agricultural region known as the Nile Delta. Antiquities ministers revealed that many treasures were under threat from building works and rising ground water levels.

Advanced techniques

- **In the past,** mummies have been badly damaged by archaeologists doing research. Today, scientists use endoscopy instead of conducting an autopsy.

- **Bone X-rays** have enabled scientists to calculate height, age at death and if the person suffered any fractures during their lifetime.

- **In 1977**, an international team began fieldwork at Giza, Saqqara, and Luxor using geographical techniques such as acoustic sounding and magnetometry.

- **Aerial photography** and thermal infrared imagery techniques have yielded results at Giza, Saqqara and Luxor.

- **A hieroglyphic text** processing programme has been developed in Holland and is now relied upon by Egyptologists around the world.

- **Radar technology** has been used to confirm the existence of a secret chamber in the Great Pyramid of Khufu at Giza.

- **Medical science** is being used to help solve the mystery of who killed Tutankhamun. An X-ray has been carried out on the pharaoh's mummy.

- **On 5 January 2005,** the pharaoh's mummy was given a CAT scan to build up a three-dimensional picture of the bones.

- **The Theban Mapping Project** has created a detailed map and database of every part of Thebes.

- **The project is** also making 3-D computer models of every tomb in Thebes.

▶ *The mummy of Tutankhamun is prepared for a scan that will reveal its internal structure and show up any signs of injury or disease.*

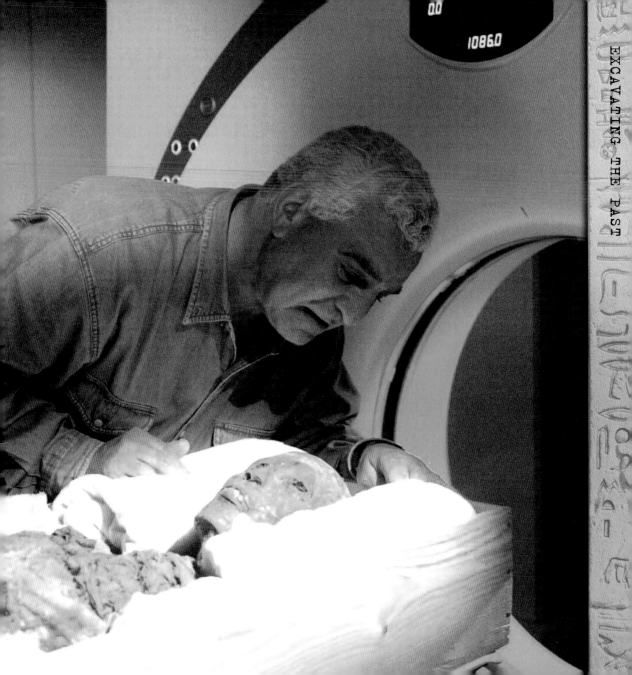

Curses and myths

- **The most famous Egyptian curse** relates to the discovery of the tomb of Tutankhamun. Carter was said to have found a tablet bearing the inscription 'Death will slay with his wings whoever disturbs the peace of the pharaoh.'

- **No trace of the tablet** has ever been found, but many of those connected with Carter's expedition died mysteriously. A few months after the tomb's opening Lord Carnarvon died at the age of 57. The exact cause of death seemed to be from an infection started by an insect bite.

- **Rumours about the mummy's curse** were fuelled when the mummy of Tutankhamun was unwrapped in 1925. It was found to have a wound on the left cheek in the same position as the fatal insect bite on Carnarvon.

- **By 1929, eleven people** connected with the discovery of the tomb had died of unnatural causes, including Carter's personal secretary and his father.

- **Carter's father committed suicide**, leaving a note that read, 'I really cannot stand any more horrors and hardly see what good I am going to do here, so I am making my exit.'

  - **Microbiologists have identified** several potentially dangerous spores that have been found in ancient tombs.

- **Scientists now wear** protective gear such as masks and gloves when unwrapping a mummy.

- **The 5th dynasty Pyramid Texts** contain a tomb curse. It reads: 'As for anyone who shall lay a finger on this pyramid and this temple which belong to me and my *ka*, …he will be one banished, one who eats himself.'

- **A curse has also been found** on the entrance to the tomb of Petety at Giza. It begins: 'Listen all of you! The priest of Hathor will beat twice any of you who enters this tomb or does harm to it.'

- **A stela belonging to Sarenput I**, a nomarch (provincial governor) under Senusret I, has a curse inscribed upon it: 'As for every mayor, every wab-priest, every scribe and every nobleman who shall take (the offering) from the statue, his arm shall be cut off like that of this bull, his neck shall be twisted off like that of a bird, his office shall not exist.'

▼ *The inner coffin of Tutankhamun, whose tomb is said to have been protected by a potent curse.*

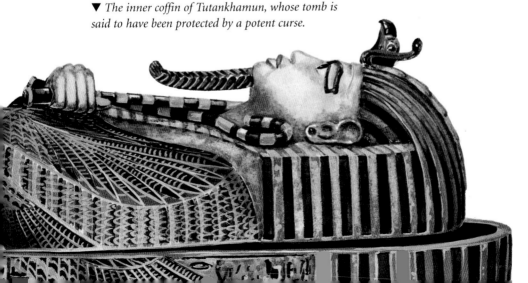

DNA and ancient Egypt

- **DNA is a material** contained in our cells that carries the genetic blueprint for life and determines hereditary characteristics. DNA testing was first developed by scientists in 1985.

- **DNA testing** is now being used to verify the family histories of pharaohs, and has helped to prove the existence of brother-sister marriages among members of the royal families.

- **To extract DNA**, scientists have to take very small samples from body tissue, hair or teeth.

- **In 1994**, Professor Scott Woodward used DNA testing on six Old Kingdom mummies. His tests indicated that two of the mummies had been put in the wrong coffins!

- **Woodward later tested 27 royal mummies** from the New Kingdom period. These samples revealed that Ahmose I had married his full sister Seknet-re.

- **The Manchester Museum in England** is the home of the International Mummy Database and Tissue Bank. Here DNA testing techniques are applied to samples of non-royal mummies from museums and institutions around the world. These reveal information about the illnesses they suffered from, and even whether there was a genetic link between different groups.

- **Dr Moamina Kamal** of Cairo University Medical School has used DNA testing to discover where the workers who built the pyramids came from. He compared samples from the workers' bones with samples taken from modern Egyptians. His results suggest that almost every family in Egypt must have been involved directly or indirectly with pyramid building.

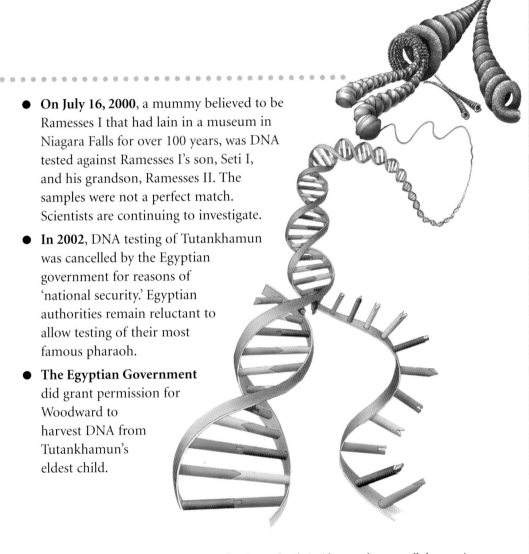

- **On July 16, 2000**, a mummy believed to be Ramesses I that had lain in a museum in Niagara Falls for over 100 years, was DNA tested against Ramesses I's son, Seti I, and his grandson, Ramesses II. The samples were not a perfect match. Scientists are continuing to investigate.

- **In 2002**, DNA testing of Tutankhamun was cancelled by the Egyptian government for reasons of 'national security.' Egyptian authorities remain reluctant to allow testing of their most famous pharaoh.

- **The Egyptian Government** did grant permission for Woodward to harvest DNA from Tutankhamun's eldest child.

▲ *DNA is the tiny molecule inside every human cell that carries genes in a code. DNA testing can help Egyptologists build a clearer picture of the correct chronology of Egyptian kings.*

Museums around the world

- **Today, there are museums** around the world displaying an incredible collection of Egyptian artefacts. Many were set up in the colonial era by European rulers.

- **The Egyptian Museum in Cairo** was established in 1835. The building in use today was constructed in 1900 and houses an incredible 120,000 items dating from the Pre-dynastic era to the Roman period.

- **The Berlin Egyptian Museum** exhibits include a 3000 year old portrait bust of Queen Nefertiti.

- **After the construction** of the High Dam at Aswan, a Nubian museum was opened in 1997, and among its thousand of artefacts are a statue of a Roman soldier, a head of King Shabatka and a statue of a Meroitic queen and prince.

- **The Gregorian Egyptian Museum** was founded by Pope Gregory XVI in 1839 with monuments and artefacts from Egypt's Imperial age.

- **The Carnegie Museum of Natural History** in Pittsburgh, United States, has dedicated the Walton Hall to Egyptian ceramic and stone vessels, jewellery, stone carvings and relief fragments, tools, and much more. There are over 2500 ancient Egyptian artefacts dating back to 3100 BC.

> **...FASCINATING FACT...**
> The British Museum holds one of the most spectacular collections of ancient Egyptian material outside Cairo including a range of coffins and mummies spanning 5000 years of history.

▲ *The Louvre Museum's Department of Egyptian Antiquities contains thousands of artefacts dating from the Pre-dynastic era to the arrival of Christianity in Roman Egypt.*

- **The collection of art** at the Metropolitan Museum in New York, is made up of 36,000 items dating from the Stone Age to the Roman period. More than half comes from the Museum's own work in Egypt, which began in 1906.

- **The Museum of Fine Arts** in Boston, USA, has one of the world's most important collections of Egyptian artefacts. Most of them were collected from the excavations of Dr. George A Reisner between 1905 and 1942.

- **The Department of Egyptian Antiquities** at the Musee de Louvre in France contains thousands of pieces, including a mummified cat and a detachable headrest from an Egyptian bed.

Index

Index

. . . .

Index

Index

Acknowledgements

The publishers would like to thank the following artists
whose work appears in this book:

John James/Temple Rogers, Janos Marffy, Mike Saunders,
Mike White/Temple Rogers

All other artworks are from the Miles Kelly Artwork Bank

The publishers would like to thank the following picture sources
whose photographs appear in this book:

Page 197 Guy_Levy/epa/CORBIS
Page 201 Supreme Council Of Antiquities/epa/CORBIS

All other photographs from:

Castrol, CMCD, Corbis, Corel, digitalSTOCK, digitalvision
Flat Earth, Hemera, ILN, John Foxx, PhotoAlto, PhotoDisc
PhotoEssentials, PhotoPro, Stockbyte